TASTE OF THE
TROPICS

Susan Parkinson was born in New Zealand where she trained as a home economist and dietitian. After working in England she gained a Masters Degree in Nutrition at Cornell University in the United States. Since 1950 she has been based in the South Pacific where she has been involved in numerous projects related to food and nutrition. In Fiji she met Peggy Stacy and together they developed a mutual interest in adapting tropical foods and recipes for inclusion in international cuisine. Their first two books, *A Taste of the Tropics* (Mills and Boon, 1972) and *Pacific Islands Cookbook* (Pacific Publications, 1977), were widely used cookery books in the region and other parts of the world.

Susan Parkinson

Peggy Stacy

Adrian Mattinson has built up a wide experience in hotel management and food preparation since graduating from the Scottish Hotel School. Born in England, he followed an international career in the food and beverage departments of luxury hotels in Europe, Africa, the Caribbean and Seychelles, before moving into personnel and training. He recently left as Head of the School of Hotel and Catering Services in Suva to become Manager of a major chain of hotels based in Fiji.

His great love of food and particular interest in the development of new styles of cooking, and the adaptation of traditional cooking methods, led him to join co-authors Susan Parkinson and Peggy Stacy in updating *A Taste of the Tropics* for the Asia Pacific Books first edition of 60,000 copies.

Ron Redfern is a New Zealand commercial photographer who has worked widely in the tropics on various commissions including photographing the recipes for *A Taste of the Tropics.* He has his own studio in Wellington where he is specialising in food photography.

Peggy Stacy received a Bachelor of Science Degree in Home Economics from Montreal, Canada, and a Diploma in Dietetics from Seattle, USA. She is the author of *The Best Australian Cookbook for Diabetics and the Overweight* which has already sold 30,000 copies. She co-authored *A Taste of the Tropics* and *Pacific Islands Cookbook* and has written numerous articles on cooking for the *Fiji Times.* Peggy Stacy is now a private consultant dietitian in Perth, Australia, and is currently working on a nutrition book about food that is low fat, low sugar and salt, and high in fibre. The book includes dietary analysis for each recipe.

Adrian Mattinson

First published 1985
This edition published 1989

© 1989 Susan Parkinson
Peggy Stacy
Adrian Mattinson

ISBN 0-947199-14-4

INTERNATIONAL DISTRIBUTORS
DINKUM FARE BOOKS

USA
T.B. Clarke (USA) Inc
150 North Autumn Street,
SAN JOSE, CA 95110 USA
Ph: (408) 298-3322 Fax: (408) 286-3077

UNITED KINGDOM
T.B. Clarke (UK) Distributors Ltd
Beckett House,
14 Billing Road,
NORTHAMPTON, UK NN1 5AW
Ph: (0604) 230-941 Fax: (0604) 230-942

SOUTH PACIFIC, SOUTH EAST ASIA
T.B. Clarke (Overseas) Pty Ltd
302 Bronte Road,
WAVERLEY, NSW. 2024, AUSTRALIA
Ph: (02) 389-8488 Fax: (02) 387-7623

AUSTRALIA
Gordon and Gotch Limited
25–37 Huntingdale Road,
BURWOOD, VIC 3125
Ph: (03) 285-1700

NEW ZEALAND
David Bateman Ltd
32–34 View Road,
Glenfield, AUCKLAND.

Published by David Bateman Ltd
Australia and New Zealand

Printed and Bound in Hong Kong

TASTE OF THE TROPICS

This exciting cookbook brings you a taste of life in the beautiful tropics with over 200 healthy and nutritious new recipes to share with your family and friends.

Hors d'Oeuvres

Making your own hors d'oeuvres is not as difficult or as time consuming as you may think. And they taste so much better.

Pastry or choux pastry cases and fried bread canapes may all be made several days ahead and stored in air-tight tins. Savoury butters keep well in the refrigerator or freezer.

A basic white sauce, made the day before and chilled, may be mixed with a variety of different flavourings and spooned into the prepared cases on the day of the party.

Savouries requiring last minute baking or grilling can also be made well ahead and deep frozen. These may then be popped in the oven, under the griller or into the microwave just before serving.

Fillings for Pastry Cases

Patty or vol-au-vent cases may be filled wih any of the following mixtures based on a plain white sauce. Allow 1 teaspoon of mixture per case. These mixtures also make delicious pancake fillings.

BASIC WHITE SAUCE

3 tablespoons butter
3 tablespoons flour
½ clove crushed garlic
½ teaspoon salt
dash of pepper
¼ teaspoon dry mustard
1 cup milk

Melt butter in a saucepan and briefly saute garlic. Stir in flour, salt, pepper and dry mustard. Slowly stir in milk and cook over low heat until thick and smooth. Allow to simmer 3 minutes. Makes 1½ cups.

CHILLI CRAB

1½ cups white sauce
1 cup cooked or canned crab
1 large clove garlic
(finely chopped)
1 tablespoon butter
2 teaspoons chilli sauce
2 teaspoons lemon juice
2 tablespoons parsley
(finely chopped)
salt to taste

Prepare basic white sauce. Coarsely flake flesh of canned crab. Saute garlic in butter, stir in crab and cook for 3 minutes. Add chilli sauce, lemon juice and finely chopped parsley. Cook for 1 minute more. Stir in sauce and check seasoning for salt. Makes 2 cups.

SEAFOOD DILL

Using whole prawns

1½ cups white sauce
½ cup cooked prawns
(or white fish)
1 teaspoon fresh dill chopped
(or ½ teaspoon dried)
2 teaspoons lemon juice
pepper to taste
chilli sauce to taste
(optional)
1 tablespoon celery or cucumber
(finely chopped)
salt to taste

Prepare basic white sauce and prawns or white fish. Season

4

Left to right: Seafood dill with whole prawns, Pacific Island filling, Petite drumsticks, Chilli crab

sauce with dill, lemon juice, pepper and chilli sauce. Stir in prawns or fish. Just before serving add celery or cucumber and season to taste with salt. Makes 2 cups.

SOUTH SEAS FILLING

1 cup coconut cream
2 teaspoons cornflour
2 or 3 teaspoons lemon juice
½ teaspoon salt
dash chilli sauce
(tabasco can be used)
1 teaspoon dill (freshly chopped)
or ¼ teaspoon dill seed
½ cup cooked prawns or
marinated fish
¼ cup raw cucumber cubes
(optional)

Prepare coconut cream according to instruction on page 93. Mix cornflour with a little of the coconut cream. Stir into remaining cream in saucepan. Bring to boiling point, stirring constantly, but do not allow to boil. Cool and add lemon juice, salt, tabasco or chilli sauce and dill. Stir in prawns or fish and cucumber.
Makes 2 cups

EGGPLANT 'CAVIAR'

An excellent vegetarian spread

1 large eggplant
1 tablespoon oil
1 small clove garlic crushed
1 to 2 teaspoons lemon juice
salt
freshly ground black pepper

Bake eggplant in a slow oven until soft (about ½ hour). Scoop the flesh out of the skin. Heat oil and saute garlic. Add eggplant and simmer for a few minutes, stirring occasionally. Season with lemon juice, salt and freshly ground black pepper. Allow to cool.
Makes 1 cup.

FRENCH TOAST

French toast is an excellent base on which to serve pate and other spreads. Slice as thinly as you can a fresh loaf of white bread or make as many slices as you think you may need. Trim off the crusts to make the pieces square and place individually on a biscuit tray in a slow oven. Cook till light golden and allow to cool before using.

PATE

Keeps well in the refrigerator and may be frozen. For those special occasions try the pate mould.

500gms (1lb) lambs fry
2 rashers bacon
freshly ground black pepper
250 gms (8oz) butter
½ small clove garlic crushed
½ teaspoon grated nutmeg
½ cup brandy
1 teaspoon sugar
salt and pepper

Variation

1. 250 gm (8 oz) lamb, beef or pig liver and 250 gms minced pork or veal.
2. 250 gms (8 oz) chicken liver and 250 gms minced pork or beef.

Remove the skin and any tough blood vessels from the liver. Place meats in a casserole, cover with bacon rashers and if using chicken livers, check to see all of the gall bladder has been removed and season with freshly ground black pepper. Cover and bake in slow oven for ¾ hour. Cool and put through a mincer twice, or reduce to a fine pulp in the blender.
Cream butter with garlic, nutmeg, brandy and sugar. Beat in pureed liver mixture or if using a blender, simply blend all ingredients at the same time. The liver blends more easily if a little additional stock is added. Check pate for flavour and add salt and pepper to taste. Place in a container and chill well.
Makes 2 cups.

Variation: Pate Moulds

½ cup water
2 teaspoons gelatine
1 beefstock cube
sliced stuffed olives

Dissolve gelatine in cold water and then add beefstock cube. Bring to the boil, stirring until liquid is clear. Arrange sliced stuffed olives on the bottom of 3 to 4 small moulds. Cover the bottom of the moulds with gelatine stock and cool. Fill with prepared pate and chill until ready to serve.

Serve surrounded by cracker biscuits or French toast.

PETITE DRUMSTICKS

1 kg (2 lb) chicken wings (10)
2 eggs (well beaten)
4 tablespoons flour
1 teaspoon salt
1 tablespoon dry sherry
oil for frying
black pepper to taste

Cut wings into joints, removing the tips. Separate the two bones in the first section with a sharp knife. You now have three bones with flesh attached. With the knife tip, lift the flesh off the bones and push this to the end of the bones to form a little drumstick. One chicken will yield 6 drumsticks.
Prepare a batter with eggs, flour, salt and dry sherry. Dip the meat end of the drumstick in batter and fry until golden in very hot deep oil. Just before serving, sprinkle with freshly ground black pepper. Serve hot or cold.
Makes about 30 drumsticks

RED BEAN

A good vegetarian spread.

1 small onion finely chopped
1 clove garlic crushed
1 tablespoon oil
1 cup cooked or canned kidney beans (reserve liquid)
1 tablespoon tomato paste or 2 of tomato puree
1 teaspoon chopped fresh basil (½ teaspoon if dry)
salt to taste
1 tablespoon sherry (optional)

Saute onion and garlic in oil until soft. Add kidney beans, tomato paste and basil. Simmer for 3 minutes. Puree in a blender or rub through a sieve. (Mix sherry in at this point if desired). If necessary adjust consistency by adding a little of the liquid from the beans
Makes 1½ cups.

TUNA CHEESE

1 tin (185 gm or 6oz) tuna
½ cup cheese (finely grated)
2 tablespoons stuffed olives (finely chopped)
1 teaspoon lemon juice
2 tablespoons mayonnaise
salt to taste
freshly ground black pepper

Drain and flake tuna. Mix in cheese, olives, lemon juice and mayonnaise. Season to taste with salt and black pepper.

From left: Smoked fish or tuna pate, Eggplant 'caviar', Red bean with French toast

SMOKED FISH or TUNA PATE

If smoked tuna is not available, substitute any other smoked fish.

250 gms (8 oz) smoked tuna
1 cup coconut cream
1 small chilli
(or ½ teaspoon tabasco sauce)
1 tablespoon lemon juice
1 teaspoon gelatine
2 teaspoons water
salt and pepper to taste

Remove skin and bones from cooked smoked tuna. Mix with coconut cream, finely chopped chilli, lemon juice and freshly ground pepper and salt in a food processor or blender until well combined but not reduced to a puree. Dissolve gelatine in water, then add to tuna. Mix well then place in serving dish and chill. Serve on biscuits or brown bread.
Makes 1½ cups

TARO CHEESE BISCUITS

1 cup grated cooked taro
1 cup flour
¼ teaspoon salt
pinch of chilli powder
90 gms (3 oz)butter
60 gms (2 oz) cheese
iced water — about 2 tablespoons

Cook taro the day before and allow to become a little dry. Grate on coarse grater. Combine flour, salt, chilli in a bowl. Add the butter and cut into the flour with two knives until it looks like breadcrumbs. Stir in the grated taro and grated cheese with a fork. Slowly add chilled water and stir with a fork till the damp mixture sticks together - it must not be too sticky. Form into a ball and roll out on floured surface, fold and wrap in paper and chill for an hour or so. Finally, roll out very thinly on floured surface. Cut into squares or rounds, put onto a floured oven sheet and bake in a hot oven till crisp and golden brown. Serve as a savoury with drinks.

NIMKIES

Nimkies are savoury biscuits. Excellent with drinks, they are best when served hot.

1 cup coarse or wholemeal flour
1 teaspoon baking powder
½ teaspoon salt
½ teaspoon cumin
¼ teaspoon turmeric
¼ teaspoon chilli powder
2 tablespoons butter or ghee
cold water
oil

Sift flour together with baking powder, salt, cumin, turmeric and chilli powder. Rub in ghee or butter. Add cold water to make a stiff dough similar to pastry. Roll out very thin on a floured surface. Cut into small attractive shapes and leave to dry for 10 minutes.
Fry in very hot fat until puffy and golden. Serve hot, or store in an airtight container.

SAMOSA

Crisp savouries with a spicy vegetable filling. Use the pastry for Nimkies. Roll out and cut into 6 cm (3 in) squares. Prepare filling as follows:-

¾ cup mashed potato
(or cooked sieved dhal)
¼ cup peas or other cooked green vegetable
1 teaspoon curry powder
½ clove crushed garlic
2 teaspoons lemon juice
salt and pepper

Mix all ingredients together. Beat well. Put spoonfuls on squares. Fold over and seal edges with water. Deep fry as for Nimkies.

Samosas

Dips & Chips

Dips and chips make ideal accompaniments to drinks and can be tasty and nutritious. They are easily made on the day or prepared in advance.

Delicious, crisp chips can be made from many starchy roots and fruits available from the tropics.

The chips should be fried in very hot flavourless salad oil, using a heavy deep saucepan. After cooking, they should be lifted out and put in a strainer to remove surplus oil and then placed in absorbent paper. Alternatively, use a frying basket. The thick type of chips should be kept hot and served as soon as possible. Thin chips may be cooled and stored in a sealed container for future use.

THIN CHIPS

Thin chips may be made from sweet potato, green bananas and cooking bananas. Green bananas should be peeled like a potato using a paring knife. Rub a little oil on the hands to prevent staining.

Cut very thin slices of your chosen vegetable with a potato peeler or a very sharp knife. Soak slices in a bowl of water for ½ an hour to draw out excess starch. Take out and dry on a cloth. Fry in deep hot oil, drain and dust with salt and pepper just before serving. Do not add salt ahead of time as chips are inclined to go soft.

THICK CHIPS

Thick chips may be made from cooked taro, breadfruit, cassava, or sweet potato. Bake, boil, or steam any of these vegetables till soft, but still firm. Cut into pieces about 1.5 to 4 cm (1 to 1½ in) long and 0.5 cm (¼ in) thick. Fry in hot oil till crisp and golden brown. Dust with salt and pepper or chilli powder.

If none of the above vegetables is available, use potato but do not pre-cook before frying.

CASSAVA DROPS

Grate raw cassava on a fine grater and season with salt and pepper. Form into small round balls by gently rolling in the hands. Drop into hot oil and fry until golden brown.

Just before serving they may be sprinkled with additional salt or a little curry powder, ground cumin, basil or any other desired spices or herbs.

TARO CHIPS

The texture of taro is such that it makes a much crisper chip. Peel taro and cut in long strips approximately 1-2 cm (¾ in) wide. Rinse well, soak in ice cold water, then dry thoroughly on cloth. Heat fat in deep heavy saucepan and when oil is very hot (plunge one chip into oil to test) put rest of chips into oil. Cook until crisp and golden. Drain on kitchen paper, sprinkle with salt and serve immediately.

GUACAMOLE

A traditional Mexican dish. Makes a lovely green creamy dip for corn chips or your favourite snack biscuits.

1 large avocado
¼ cup cream cheese
⅓ cup mayonnaise
½ teaspoon chilli powder
2 teaspoons minced onion
1 small clove garlic, crushed
2 teaspoons lemon juice
1 medium sized tomato
salt to taste

Peel and mash avocado. Blend with cream cheese, mayonnaise, chilli powder, onion, garlic, lemon juice and tomato which has been peeled, seeded and chopped. Mix well and season to taste with salt. Stand for 1 hour before serving to allow flavour to develop. Serve with crackers or corn chips.

Makes 2 cups.

COCONUT, FISH & GARLIC

To reduce calories substitute non-fat yoghurt for the sour cream.

1 teaspoon lime or lemon juice
¼ cup firmly packed freshly grated coconut
(or ½ cup desiccated coconut)
½ cup finely flaked cooked white fish
1 small clove garlic, crushed
½ cup sour cream
salt and pepper

Add lemon or lime juice, coconut, flaked fish and a clove of garlic to the sour cream. Season to taste with salt and pepper. Mix well. Refrigerate for 2 hours before serving to allow the full flavour to develop.
Makes 1½ cups

COCONUT CHEESE (KORA)

Kora, or fermented coconut is a traditional Fijian dish which must use fresh coconut. It has a fresh cheese-like flavour and can be served with fish, or on biscuits.

1 fresh coconut grated
1 extra coconut
1 cup boiled water with ½ teaspoon salt added
pepper or chopped chillies to taste
2 teaspoons lemon juice
1 teaspoon grated onion

Squeeze the cream from 1 freshly grated coconut. (See page 93). Mix the grated flesh with the boiled salted water. Put in a jar, cover and leave in a warm place. Stir daily for one week. At the end of the fermentation period the coconut should have a soft smooth consistency. Strain off the liquid. Squeeze the cream from another grated coconut (do not add water). Mix the cream with the fermented coconut flesh, flavour with pepper or chopped chillies, lemon juice and grated onion.
Makes 1 cup

YOGHURT & CUCUMBER

A good dip which may also be used as an accompaniment to curry or pilau.

½ medium sized cucumber
½ teaspoon salt
1 cup yoghurt
½ clove garlic, crushed
½ teaspoon salt
1 teaspoon fresh chopped dill
(or ½ teaspoon dry)

Peel and grate cucumber, sprinkle with salt and leave to drain in a strainer. Mix garlic, salt and dill into yoghurt. Stir in cucumber and chill well.
Makes 2 cups

Dips clockwise from bottom left: Taro chips Yoghurt and cucumber Guacamole, Coconut fish and garlic

Cocktails & Sauces

MARINATED FISH (KOKODA)

A fish with a fine but firm white flesh and not too many bones is best. The coconut sauce should be delicately flavoured with onion, lemon, a little chilli and, possibly ginger or dill. Unless told, most people would not realise that this is raw fish. Highly recommended.

750 gms (1½ lbs) white fish
1 cup lime or lemon juice
2 medium sized coconuts
(or 3 cups desiccated coconut and 1 cup warm milk)
1 lemon
1 small sliced onion
1 chopped chilli
1 teaspoon salt
1 cup water

(omit water if using desiccated coconut)

Remove the bones and skin from the fish and cut into 2 cm (1 in) cubes. Place in a bowl, cover with lime or lemon juice and leave for about 2 hours. Grate coconuts, cut lemon into wedges, onion into

Top: Kokoda (Marinated fish). Left: Prawn and avocado cocktail   Right: Indian spiced vegetable salad.

slices, and chop chilli. Combine grated coconut with above ingredients and season with salt. Add one cup water, stir well with hands and squeeze out the cream and strain. If using desiccated coconut add the warm milk at this stage and omit water. After 2 hours strain fish and discard juice. Pour the flavoured coconut cream over the fish and garnish with grated carrot, tomato and lemon slices. Serve in chilled glass dishes.
Makes 6 to 8 ½-cup servings

Variation

Add one tablespoon fresh dill or 2 teaspoons finely chopped fresh ginger to coconut with lemon and onion. Do not cool to very low temperatures as this will make the coconut cream granular.

AVOCADO with CHILLI TOMATO SAUCE

Avocado has the distinction of providing more calories than any other fruit. This is due to the fat content which makes it smooth and creamy.

3 ripe, but firm avocados
2-3 tablespoons lemon juice
1 medium sized tomato
3 teaspoons chilli sauce
1 teaspoon sugar
2 tablespoons finely chopped spring onion
½ cup mayonnaise
salt to taste

Cut avocados in half and remove the stones. Sprinkle liberally with lemon juice to prevent discoloration. Chill thoroughly. Just before serving fill cavity with the following sauce.

Sauce

Peel, seed and finely chop the tomato. Add chilli sauce, sugar and finely chopped spring onions and tomato to the mayonnaise. Season to taste with salt. Refrigerate for at least two hours before serving to allow the full flavour to develop.
Serves 6

CAVIAR AVOCADO

Perfect for that special dinner party

3 ripe avocados
2-3 tablespoons lemon juice
1 teaspoon salt
2 cloves garlic
½ cup caviar (or lumpfish roe)
parsley to garnish

Cut avocados in half and remove the stones. Sprinkle liberally with lemon juice to prevent discoloration and then sprinkle the surface with salt and the juice from the crushed garlic. Place about 2 teaspoons of caviar in each cavity. Garnish with a sprig of parsley and serve well-chilled on a bed of lettuce.
Serves 6

KOKODA with PRAWNS

This tasty dish using marinated fish with prawns is an ideal entree for a formal dinner.

500 gms (1 lb) white fish
1 cup lemon or lime juice
250 gms (8 oz) cooked and peeled prawns
½ medium sized cucumber
basic coconut cream sauce
1 teaspoon chopped dill

Prepare and marinate fish for two hours in lemon or lime juice as directed in basic recipe. Cook and peel prawns and then cut into ½ cm (¼ in) pieces. Peel and dice cucumber. Prepare coconut cream sauce as directed in basic recipe, adding chopped dill as an additional flavouring.
Serves 6

WATERMELON SEAFOOD MOUSSE

Rock melon, honeydew melon, or even apple may be substituted in this recipe.

1 tablespoon gelatine
¼ cup cold water
¾ cup finely chopped celery
1½ cups cooked flaked seafood (fish, prawns, etc)
1 cup cubed watermelon
½ cup mayonnaise
2 tablespoons lemon juice
salt to taste
freshly ground pepper
½ cup whipped fresh cream

Soak gelatine in cold water, then place over hot water to dissolve. Mix dissolved gelatine, chopped celery, prepared seafood and watermelon together. Moisten with mayonnaise and then season with lemon juice, salt and pepper. Fold in whipped cream. Pour into small individual moulds or a 4-cup mould and refrigerate until set. Unmould onto a bed of watercress or lettuce. Use pieces of watermelon, or slices of lime or lemon and chopped parsley as garnish.
Serves 6

Cocktail Sauces

AVOCADO SAUCE

1 medium ripe avocado
½ clove garlic
2 teaspoons finely chopped onion
3 teaspoons lemon juice
½ teaspoon salt or to taste
½ - 1 teaspoon chilli sauce
1 cup evaporated milk

Sieve or blend ripe avocado. Crush ½ clove of garlic. Mix onion, garlic, lemon juice, salt, and chilli sauce into the avocado. Beat in evaporated milk. Serve well-chilled with grapefruit, oranges, bananas and celery, or with watermelon or seafood.
Serves 6

SEAFOOD SAUCE

A delightful sauce, to be used with any seafood combination. Try it with prawns, crab, or crayfish, along with some chopped celery and lettuce.

⅓ **cup mayonnaise**
¼ **cup tomato sauce**
½ **teaspoon Worcestershire sauce**
1½ **teaspoons lemon juice**
dash of cayenne pepper or chilli sauce
salt and pepper to taste

Combine mayonnaise with tomato sauce, Worcestershire sauce, lemon juice, cayenne pepper and salt and pepper to taste. Serve with any desired combination of seafood.
Makes ⅔ cup

Watermelon seafood mousse

Soups

Good stock is the basis of all fine soups. It is worth while keeping a supply deep frozen. If home-made bone stock is not available, you can make quite a good substitute by boiling stock powder or cubes with the correct amount of water and adding vegetables and herbs.

Many soups are equally good served hot or cold. For hot weather menus we have included a number which are chilled. The success of a chilled soup depends on serving it very cold. Just a few degrees above freezing point is best. To achieve this, soup bowls or cups must be thoroughly cooled before the meal, or arranged on a bed of crushed ice. Freeze a little of the soup mixture in an ice-cube tray and put a cube or ball in each serving.

Cold soups need to be more highly seasoned than hot soups, as chilling dulls the sense of taste. At the hot stage the mixture should taste a little over seasoned. When cold it will be just right.

Soups may be served with colourful and tasty garnishes. These may vary from chopped crisp cucumber, thin slices of tomato, to crisp bacon crumbs, toasted sesame seeds or fried cubes of bread.

Avocado soup

AVOCADO SOUP

1 cup mashed avocado
1 small clove garlic
1 teaspoon salt
1 tablespoon lemon juice
¼ teaspoon chilli sauce
600 ml (1 pint) chicken stock
600 ml (1 pint) milk
lemon slices
chives
caviar or lumpfish roe

Sieve or puree ripe avocado. Season with juice from garlic, salt, lemon juice and chilli sauce. Add stock and milk to avocado mixture and beat until a creamy consistency is reached. Serve well chilled with a slice of lemon, chopped chives or a little caviar.
Note: This soup may also be served hot but care should be taken to heat gently without allowing to boil.
Serves 6-8

TOMATO HERB SOUP

1 kg (2 lb) tomatoes
1 clove garlic
1 small onion
1½ tablespoons oil
1 teaspoon fresh chopped mint
½ teaspoon fresh chopped basil
1 teaspoon chopped parsley
½ teaspoon chopped marjoram
3 cups beef stock

Coconut fish soup

2 teaspoons sugar
salt
1 tablespoon cornflour
2 tablespoons water
cream
spring onion or mint to garnish

Peel tomatoes and chop, crush garlic, chop onion finely. Put oil in large saucepan, heat and saute onion and garlic till golden. Add tomatoes and stir well. Season with chopped herbs such as mint, basil, parsley and marjoram. Simmer 5 minutes and then add stock, sugar and salt. Cover and simmer for 20 minutes. Strain and measure. Add extra stock if needed to make six servings. Mix corn-

Tomato herb soup

ful of coconut cream and chopped chives. Serves 6

EGGPLANT SOUP

This eggplant or aubergine soup may be served hot or cold

1 medium onion
1 rasher of bacon
1 clove of garlic
2 teaspoons coriander seeds
(or ½ teaspoon ground)
2 tablespoons oil
½ kg (1 lb) eggplant
5-6 cups beef stock
green coriander or parsley
6 tablespoons yoghurt

Finely chop onion and bacon, crush garlic. Heat oil and saute onion, bacon, garlic, and coriander for a few minutes. Peel and slice the eggplants and add to onion mixture. Cook for a further 5 minutes. Add beef stock and simmer for 20-30 minutes with lid on saucepan. Blend or sieve the mixture. Measure to see that there are the required number of servings and, if necessary, add extra stock. Adjust flavour and serve hot or chilled. (If serving chilled, remember to slightly overseason as chilling tends to dull the flavours). Garnish with chopped green coriander or parsley and a spoonful of yoghurt.
Serves 5-6

MUSSEL SOUP

This soup can be from any sea or river shellfish.

2 dozen small mussels (1 doz large)
375 gms (12 oz) any similar shellfish
1 medium onion
600 ml (1 pint) water
600 ml (1 pint) milk
tabasco sauce
1 teaspoon salt
4 tablespoons butter
4 tablespoons flour
4 teaspoons lemon juice
chopped chives or green onion
lemon slices

flour with water and stir into soup. Serve hot or chilled topped with a spoonful of cream and chopped herbs.
Serves 6

LEAFY GREEN SOUP

A delicious cream soup using a variety of green leafy vegetables.

250 gms (8 oz) green leaf vegetables
(spinach, watercress, lettuce, taro, Chinese cabbage)
½ medium onion
water
salt
4 tablespoons butter
1 clove garlic, crushed
¼ teaspoon curry powder
4 tablespoons flour
3 cups milk
3 cups chicken stock
salt and pepper to taste

tabasco sauce (optional)
¼ teaspoon grated lemon rind
6 tablespoons coconut cream
chopped chives or spring onion

Prepare the green leaves and onions and cook in boiling salted water for 5-10 minutes or till just tender. This is important in order to retain colour and food value. Strain, puree and sieve. Melt butter, add garlic and curry powder and saute for a minute. Stir in flour and cook for a minute then gradually add the milk and stock stirring all the time. Add grated lemon rind and tabasco sauce. Boil for a few minutes, add the green puree, check for flavour. Serve hot or chilled garnished with a spoon-

Mussel soup

Prepare shellfish by pouring over boiling water or putting in the deep freeze. Either method makes it simple to open the shells. Remove flesh and put in a saucepan with ¼ of the onion, water and salt. Bring to the boil and simmer 10 minutes. Strain and reserve stock. Put the shellfish in a blender or mincer. If necessary sieve to remove muscle fibres. Mix fish puree with stock and add milk and a few drops of tabasco sauce. Chop remaining onion finely. Melt butter and fry the onion till soft, stir in the flour and cook for a minute. Remove from heat and slowly stir in the stock and milk. Bring to boiling point stirring all the time. Simmer for 5 minutes. Add extra salt if needed. Just before serving slowly add lemon juice. Serve garnished with thin slices of lemon and chopped chives or green onion.
Serves 6

COCONUT FISH SOUP

1 kg (2 lbs) fish, or fish heads
7 cups of water
2 teaspoons salt
1 large onion
black pepper
1 chilli (optional)
2 cups thick coconut cream
1 tablespoon lemon juice
lemon slices
chopped spring onion

Put fish in a large saucepan with water, salt, pepper, onion and chilli. Bring slowly to simmering point and maintain till fish is soft. Cool and strain off stock. Taste for flavour and add extra seasoning if needed. Heat, and just before serving, stir in lemon juice and coconut cream. Do not boil after cream has been added. Serve garnished with a slice of lemon and some chopped green onion.
Serves 6

DHAL SOUP

This easy to make spicy soup is widely used in India. Try varying the flavour by using different spices such as cardamom, coriander, turmeric and curry leaf

1½ cups dhal
(split peas or other dried legumes)
6 cups water or stock
1 teaspoon salt
1 tablespoon oil or ghee
¼ teaspoon crushed green ginger
(or pinch teaspoon cumin seed
1 teaspoon curry powder
1 small onion finely chopped
1 small onion finely chopped
extra water or stock
chopped fresh mint or coriander leaves

Wash dhal and soak for an hour in water or stock. Add salt and cook till soft. Remove the white forth which forms during boiling. Measure, and add enough stock or water to make 6 cups of soup. Heat the oil or ghee in a pan and add crushed ginger, cumin and curry powder. Stir for a minute and then add onion. Saute for a few minutes over low heat. Add a little soup to the spices in the pan and cook for a minute. Return spices to the soup and simmer 5 minutes. Stir well and serve garnished with chopped fresh mint or coriander leaves.

Variation

For a smoother texture, strain soup and put the dhal in a blender.

CUCUMBER SOUP

Delicious hot or cold

1 clove garlic
375 gm (12 oz) cucumber
  (dark green)
1 small onion
3 tablespoons butter
3 tablespoons flour
4 cups chicken stock
2 cups milk
salt to taste
1 teaspoon lemon juice
sour cream or yoghurt
dill or chopped parsley

Crush the garlic with ¼ teaspoon salt. Cut up the cucumber leaving the skin on. Put the butter in a pot and heat. Add the garlic and onion and saute a few minutes, then add the cucumber and saute another 5 minutes. Do not allow to brown. Stir the flour into the vegetables and cook for a few minutes. Now slowly add the chicken stock and milk. Stir till boiling and allow to simmer until cucumber is soft. Cook for as short a time as possible to retain the green colour. Strain off the vegetables and blend till smooth or sieve. If a mature fruit has been used it may be necessary to strain blended cucumber. Combine cucumber puree and liquid. Season to taste.

Serve the soup hot or chilled. Just before serving stir in 1 teaspoon of lemon juice. Garnish with a little sour cream or yoghurt and chopped dill or parsley.
Serves 6

Note: This soup should be a pale green colour. To achieve this use a dark green cucumber or add a few spinach leaves when cooking the cucumber.

Cucumber soup

18

Salads

Salads are a delicious and healthy way of using a variety of raw, lightly-blanched and cooked vegetables. They may be served before, during or straight after a main course. Substantial salads using meat or fish as well as vegetables can be meals in themselves.

The success of a salad depends on the combination of flavours and textures. Try combining raw and blanched fresh vegetables and use a variety of dressings. Most salads benefit from a good dressing. It is a good idea to keep one or two basic dressings in bottles in the refrigerator. Different flavourings may then be added to suit the salad of the day.

Nearly all the tropical starchy roots and fruits may be used to replace potato in salads. Most of these have a better flavour when cooked in the skin. Steam bake or remove the skin and then cube or slice.

Tropical Green Salads
Interesting salads can be made from a number of lightly-blanched vegetable shoots and stems. These can be used on their own or combined with lettuce, raw spinach, Chinese cabbage, watercress and many other well-known salad vegetables.

Young Taro or Beet Stems
Carefully peel off the outer skin, cut the stalks into 10 cm (4 inch) lengths, tie in bundles, plunge into boiling water and cook rapidly for 2-3 minutes. Remove, cool and shred with a sharp knife. Serve with lemon juice or a dressing or combine with raw carrot and other green vegetables.

Pumpkin Tops
Select the young tops of vines and prepare as above.

Fern Fronds
The young stems and furled tops of edible ferns make a delicious salad. Break off the top tender section of the stalk, cut in four, cook as above and serve with coconut cream or French dressing.

Use fern fronds with other leafy green vegetables such as creeping or English spinach, Chinese cabbage, red chicory, and watercress.

Bean Sprouts
The sprouts of a number of beans and peas make delicious, crisp salads. These can be grown at home in a jar, in a warm place, or bought fresh. Wash well, dry in a cloth and serve plain or mixed.

Breadfruit
Punch a breadfruit with a skewer several places. Put in the oven at 180ºC (350ºF) and bake for about an hour. Test with skewer to see if breadfruit is soft.

Sweet Potato
Scrub well and then steam or boil until soft. When cool, remove skin. (See Spiced Sweet Potato and Banana Salad page 22).

Taro
Peel first, then steam or boil until soft. Cube and use as for potato in potato salads.

Yam
Puncture with a skewer then bake or steam in the skin, or peel and boil.

Cooking Banana (Plantain)
Boil or steam, and then peel. Combine with sweet potato and mayonnaise to make Spiced Sweet Potato and Banana Salad page 22.

MIXED GREEN SALAD

250 gms (4 oz) Chinese cabbage
leaves and stalks
250 gms spinach leaves
250 gms watercress
250 gms other greens
(sweet potato vine tips etc)
½ cup chopped parsley or
spring onion or chopped herbs
1 cup bean sprouts

Wash leaves well, shake dry and
put in a plastic bag in the
refrigerator to crisp. Shred the cabbage, tear the spinach leaves, take
the tips off the cress and use the
leaves, discarding tough stems.
Use the tips of the sweet potato
vine including young whole leaves
in the salad. Add bean sprouts,
some chopped fresh herbs or a little spring onion. Toss with a well
flavoured dressing.
Note: Any other suitable leaves
may be used in roughly the same
proportions. It is important to see
that the stronger flavoured kinds
are combined with those of milder
flavour.

PRAWN RICE SALAD

24 prawns
or 500 gm (1 lb) small prawns
4 cups cooked rice
1 cup cubed celery or cucumber
2 rashers of bacon
250 gm (8 oz) mandarin or orange
segments
¼ cup grated coconut
½ cup sour cream
2 teaspoons lemon juice
salt to taste
watercress

Cut large prawns into thirds. Cut
cucumber or celery into cubes.
Finely chop bacon and fry till
golden. Mix prawns, celery, bacon,
coconut together. Combine sour
cream and lemon juice. With a fork
stir the sour cream into the rice
prawn mixture, adding salt to taste,
Chill and serve on bed of watercress.

Note: Canned mandarin and desiccated coconut may be substituted
for fresh foods.

CHINESE CABBAGE & CARROT SALAD

*Any type of cabbage may be used
but the Chinese cabbage does give
greater flavour and colour.*

1½ cups finely shredded Chinese
cabbage
1½ cups grated raw carrot
1 cup blue cheese dressing or Miti
(see page 23)

Toss shredded cabbage and raw
grated carrot together. Place 1½
cups of salad on each plate, with 2
tablespoons of blue cheese dressing or miti on top.
Serves 6

LEMON EGGPLANT SALAD

4 large eggplants
2½ cups water
½ cup salad oil
½ teaspoon coriander seed
1 teaspoon salt
½ cup lemon juice or white vinegar
fresh herbs (basil, parsley, tarragon)
1 bayleaf
½ cup currants

Peel and dice eggplant into 2 cm
(½ inch) cubes. Place water, salad
oil, coriander, salt, lemon juice,
fresh herbs, and bayleaf into a
saucepan. Bring to boil, add eggplant and simmer until just tender
(it must not be mushy). Remove eggplant and reduce liquid by half
through boiling. Strain. Add currants to liquid and simmer for 5
more minutes. Pour over cooked
eggplant and chill. Serve with
lemon slices and chopped parsley.
Serves 6

Lemon eggplant salad

20

SUNSET SALAD

A delicious salad using eggplant or aubergine as its main ingredient.

**750 gms (1½ lbs) eggplant
2 tablespoons oil
1 large onion finely chopped
1 large clove garlic crushed
1½ tablespoons oil
1½ tablespoons tomato paste
1 cup tomato juice
1½ tablespoons anchovies
1 tablespoon vinegar
1 teaspoon sugar
1 teaspoon salt
½ cup parsley finely chopped
1 cup celery finely chopped**

Peel and cut eggplant into 2 cm (1 in) cubes. Heat oil in a heavy saucepan and then saute the eggplant until soft, but not mushy. Drain well and place on absorbent paper until the sauce is ready.

Sauce

Saute onion and garlic in oil in a heavy saucepan until soft. Stir in tomato paste and tomato juice. Add chopped anchovies, vinegar, sugar, salt and parsley. Simmer for 5-10 minutes. Blanch celery in boiling water for 3 minutes. Drain and stir celery and eggplant into sauce. Serve well-chilled as an appetiser garnished with freshly chopped parsley, black olives or capers on thick slices of buttered brown bread.

Serves 6

Variation

For a more substantial dish fold in 2 cups of cold flaked tuna.

PACIFIC ISLAND FISH SALAD

**500 gms (1 lb) white fish
1 teaspoon salt
½ cup lemon juice
½ small onion chopped
1 medium carrot grated
1 medium cucumber, cubed
1 capsicum, sliced
2 cups shredded Chinese or English cabbage**

Pacific Island fish salad

**2-3 tomatoes cubed
½ cup French dressing,
(or mayonnaise, or miti)**

Cut the fish into 1 cm (½ inch) cubes and put into a bowl. Sprinkle with salt and stir well. Then cover with lemon juice and leave for two hours. Put in a strainer and squeeze out the juice. Chill. Chop the onion finely, grate the carrot, partly peel the cucumber and cut into small cubes, slice the capsicum, shred the cabbage and cut the tomatoes into cubes. Combine the fish with the vegetables and just before the meal toss in dressing, miti or mayonnaise. Serves 6

RICE SALAD

A tasty rice salad which is particularly good with seafood.

**3 cups boiled rice
2 hard-boiled eggs
2 tablespoons capers
½ cup mayonnaise
½ teaspoon caraway or fennel seed
salt and pepper to taste
1 cup finely chopped cucumber**

Prepare rice and eggs. Chop eggs and capers finely. Toss rice, egg and capers together. Add sufficient mayonnaise to moisten thoroughly. Season with caraway seeds and salt and pepper to taste. Chill, then fold in finely chopped cucumber.
Serves 6

INDIAN SPICED VEGETABLE SALAD

This simple dish provides a delicious first course to a meal and is very suitable for a vegetarian menu.

**300 gms (10 oz) okra
(or sliced zucchini)
30 gms (1 oz) tamarind
(or 1 teaspoon lemon juice)
water
1 large potato
1 large onion
1 clove garlic
3 tablespoons oil
½ tablespoon mustard seed
½ teaspoon cumin seed
¼ teaspoon chilli powder
(or 1 small seeded chilli)
1 tablespoon curry powder
2 bay leaves
(or six curry leaves)
1 teaspoon salt
2 cups cooked rice
parsley or coriander as garnish
yoghurt**

Scrape the okra and cut into 1 cm (½ inch) pieces or dice zucchini. Mix the tamarind pulp or lemon juice with the water. Peel and dice the potato, finely chop the onion, crush the garlic. Heat oil in a large saucepan and saute the spices for a minute, then add the garlic and half the onion and continue stirring all the time. When onion is clear, add remaining vegetables and saute another 5 minutes. Strain the tamarind or lemon water on to the vegetables and simmer till potato is cooked. Add extra salt if necessary. Remove bay or curry leaves before serving.
Serve chilled on lettuce leaves and garnish with a spoonful of yoghurt and chopped parsley or coriander.
Serves 6

Note: Cooking in tamarind water makes the okra go brown in colour. To brighten the salad reserve ¼ of the okra. Cook 5 minutes in boiling water, drain well and rinse under cold water and mix with vegetables just before serving.

RAITA (Yoghurt Salad)

There are many variations you may make. Serve with Pilau or curry.

**¼ medium cucumber
2 medium cooked potatoes
½ small onion
2-3 tomatoes
2 cups yoghurt
½ teaspoon salt
¼ teaspoon cumin seeds**

Peel and cube cucumber, add salt and place in a strainer and drain off any juice. Cube cooked potato and add to cucumber. Finely chop onion and tomato. Toss all together with thick plain yoghurt, add cumin seeds, and season with ½ teaspoon salt. Makes 5-6 cups.

Variations
Substitute taro, cassava or yam for potato. Green peppers or celery may be used instead of, or with, cucumber.
Add 2 tablespoons finely chopped parsley or coriander leaves.
Add 2 tablespoons finely chopped spring onions instead of onion.

SPICED SWEET POTATO & BANANA SALAD

An unusual but very delicious salad.

**500 gms (1 lb) cooked sweet potato
4 ripe bananas
¼ cup lemon juice
2 tablespoons oil
2 teaspoons curry powder
2 cloves garlic, crushed
½ cup mayonnaise
¼ cup spring onions
parsley as garnish**

Cut cooked sweet potato into 2 cm (1 in) cubes. Slice bananas and marinate in lemon juice. Heat oil in saucepan. Saute curry powder and crushed cloves of garlic. Cool and combine with mayonnaise to form curry dressing. Combine banana

and sweet potato. Fold in dressing and chopped spring onions. Garnish with chopped parsley or coriander leaves if available.
Serves 6-8

Salad Dressings

QUICK DRESSINGS
A whole range of thick and thin dressings can easily be made in a blender or with an electric or hand beater.

The basic recipe for dressings is as follows:

1 part acid - this can be vinegar, or freshly squeezed lemon or lime juice.

3 parts oil - this must be a good quality oil such as olive, corn, sunflower or chosen according to individual taste.

Remember that inferior vinegar or cooking oil will ruin the flavour of a dressing.

To the basic recipe you could add a range of seasonings that might be required, plus for slight creaminess, one egg yolk, or for thickness two egg yolks.

To prepare, always follow this routine :-

Into the blender or bowl, first place the acid. Then add the oil and all the required seasonings and additives plus the egg yolks, if used. Blend or beat quickly for about 5 seconds. Taste and adjust seasoning. The dressing is now ready and can be bottled, provided it is kept in the refrigerator.

It is a good idea to have several different dressings available to vary your salads.

BASIC FRENCH DRESSING

1 small clove garlic
1 teaspoon salt
freshly ground black pepper
1 teaspoon sugar
¼ cup lemon juice
(or wine or malt vinegar)
¾ cup good quality salad oil

Crush clove of garlic in salt, add black pepper and sugar. Beat in lemon juice or vinegar and then add salad oil. Store in jar, or bottle and shake well before using.
Makes 1 cup.

Variations

FRENCH HERB
Add 1 tablespoon of finely chopped fresh herbs to ½ cup of French dressing just before serving.

CURRY
Add 1 teaspoon of curry powder to 1 cup of French dressing.

TOMATO
Use 1 tablespoon of tomato puree and 2 tablespoons of lemon juice in the basic French dressing recipe in place of the ¼ cup lemon juice.

BLUE CHEESE
Add 60 gms (2 oz) blue cheese. Mash cheese with fork and beat into dressing. (Alternatively put all ingredients in a blender and mix till smooth.)

Dressings from left: Pawpaw seed, Mexican, Blue cheese, Banana radish
Top left: Spiced sweet potato and banana salad

MEXICAN

¼ cup red wine vinegar
¼ cup olive oil
¾ cup salad oil
¼ cup (2 oz) tomato puree
1 tablespoon chopped fresh fennel
2 cloves garlic
2 teaspoons celery salt
1 small onion
1 green capsicum, chopped
½ teaspoon chilli, chopped
½ teaspoon raw sugar
1 egg yolk

Chop onion and lightly saute in butter. Combine with rest of ingredients and blend or beat well.
Makes 1¾ cups

BANANA RADISH

An excellent dressing for cole-slaw

2 bananas
2 tablespoons white radish, grated
¼ cup mayonnaise
3 teaspoons lemon juice
¼ teaspoon salt
1 teaspoon castor sugar
¼ teaspoon Worcester sauce

Mash bananas to yield approximately 1 cup. Grate fresh white radish. Blend bananas, radish, mayonnaise. Season with lemon juice, salt, castor sugar, and Worcester sauce.
Makes 1½ cups

COCONUT CREAM (Miti)

A creamy, tangy dressing.

1 cup thick coconut cream
¼ cup lemon juice
½ teaspoon salt
1 teaspoon grated onion
½ teaspoon chopped chilli

Combine all ingredients and serve fresh. Alternatively, miti can be left to ferment for a few days. During this time it develops a stronger acid flavour.
Makes 1½ cups

SESAME OIL

Excellent for rice, bean sprouts or Chinese cabbage rolls.

⅓ cup of salad oil
⅓ cup sesame oil
2 teaspoons soy sauce
1 teaspoon prepared mustard
¼ teaspoon black pepper
⅓ cup lemon juice

Place salad oil and sesame oil in a bowl. Add soy sauce, prepared mustard, black pepper and lemon juice. Beat thoroughly.
Makes 1 cup

PAWPAW SEED

Save the seeds when using fresh pawpaw to make this delicious dressing. Serve as a sauce for fish cocktail, or fruit cocktail with equal quantities of banana, pawpaw and apple

1 tablespoon sugar
½ teaspoon salt
½ teaspoon dry mustard
½ cup malt vinegar
1 cup salad oil
2 tablespoons minced onion
1 tablespoon pawpaw seeds

Place sugar, salt, dry mustard, malt vinegar, salad oil, minced onion and pawpaw seed in the blender. Blend until a smooth creamy dressing is achieved.
Makes 2 cups

Vegetables clockwise from left: Root ginger, White radish, Eggplant, Long beans and Chillies.

Menu Specialties

SEAFOOD SPINACH QUICHE

A delicious lunch or supper dish. Taro or beet leaves can be substituted for spinach.

2 eggs
¾ cup milk
½ cup grated cheese
1 tablespoon grated onion
¾ cup of cooked chopped taro or silver beet (spinach) leaves
1 cup cooked crab meat or prawns
1 teaspoon salt
¼ teaspoon cayenne pepper
23 cm (9 in) unbaked pie shell of short crust or flaky pastry

Beat eggs with milk, add cheese, onion, chopped leaves and crab or prawns, salt and cayenne pepper. Carefully pour into 23 cm (9 in) un-baked pie shell of shortcrust pastry. Bake in a 220ºC (425ºF) oven for the first 10 minutes. Reduce heat to 160ºC (325ºF) and bake for a further 25-30 minutes. Serve immediately
Serves 5-6

CHINESE OMELET

A light and simple lunch dish

250 gms (8oz) fresh bean sprouts
1 green pepper
4 spring onions
4 tablespoons oil
8 eggs
½ cup water
½ teaspoon salt
freshly ground black pepper
1 cup cooked ham, prawns or pork

Seafood spinach quiche

COCONUT EGG CURRY

1 fresh coconut
1 tablespoon lemon juice
4 onions
3 tablespoons butter or ghee
1 teaspoon turmeric
1 teaspoon coriander
½ teaspoon chilli powder
6 hard-boiled eggs

Crack coconut and reserve water. Grate the flesh and mix with lemon juice. Thinly slice onions. Crush ¼ cup of onion slices with a wooden spoon. Fry crushed onion in butter or ghee. Add turmeric, coriander and chilli powder and stir-fry for one minute. Add grated coconut and cook for 5 minutes. Add sliced onion and coconut water and simmer till cooked. Season with salt. Slice hard-boiled eggs and place in a flat dish, cover with sauce and keep hot for 10 minutes before serving to allow flavour to penetrate. Serves 4-5

VEGETABLE CHEESE PIE

150 gm (5 oz) butter or margarine
4 large tomatoes
2 onions finely sliced
½ cup sliced mushrooms
small can asparagus pieces
salt and pepper
1½ cups mashed taro

Cheese Sauce

60 gm (2 oz) butter or margarine
¼ cup flour
1⅓ cups milk
1 cup grated cheddar cheese

Heat 50 gm butter or margarine and saute skinned chopped tomatoes, onions and mushrooms until softened. Mix with the drained asparagus pieces and seasoning.

Spoon into 4 individual dishes. Add the rest of the butter or margarine to the taro and season. Put into a piping bag with a 2 cm (¾ in) rose pipe, and pipe a border round the edge of the dishes. Make the cheese sauce by heating the butter, stir in flour and blend in the milk. Stir until thickened. Add the cheese and heat gently. Spoon sauce over the vegetables. Place in a pre-heated oven at 220º C (400º F) till golden brown, then garnish with sliced tomato.

Coconut egg curry

28

Fish

When buying whole fish ensure that eyes are bright and full, the flesh firm and the gills pink to reddish.
Shellfish, crabs and lobsters are best bought alive to ensure freshness and should be cooked and eaten as soon as possible. They are usually cooked by simmering in water, in the case of shellfish from only a few minutes to about 15 to 20 minutes for lobsters.
To obtain the meat from cooked crabs, allow to cool and then cut down the centre of the underside and pull back the soft shell. Scoop the flesh out and then crack the legs and claws. (Keep some of the legs intact for garnishing.) Flake the flesh with a fork or serve in pieces. The amount of flesh obtained from crabs depends on the species, the season and the sex. In general female crabs have more flesh. Canned crab meat makes a good substitute for fresh.
The best seasonings for fish dishes are coriander, marjoram, savory, thyme, dill, mace, fennel, clove, tarragon, mint, parsley, pepper. For shellfish, try tarragon, mustard seed, garlic, oregano, paprika, sweet basil.

Fried spiced fish

FRIED SPICED FISH

Something a little different from the usual.

1 kg (2 lb) fish fillets
milk
½ cup flour
1 teaspoon salt
2 teaspoons curry powder
oil
1½ cups coconut cream

Cut fish into servings, dip in milk and then in flour mixed with curry powder and salt. Heat oil and fry on both sides till golden brown. Either heat coconut cream and serve as an accompaniment or place fish in baking dish, cover with coconut cream and bake in moderate oven for 15-20 minutes. Serve with lemon or lime slices, rice and salad.
Serves 5-6

SLICED COLD FISH

An excellent summer luncheon dish

1½ kg (3 lb) firm fleshed fish (tuna, mackerel, cod)
2 tablespoons lemon juice
1 teaspoon salt
sprig of dill or parsley
2½ cups water
1 small onion
1 bay leaf
4-6 black peppercorns
lemon slices

Remove the skin from a mid section of a fish. Place fish in a casserole and add lemon juice, water, salt and dill. Slice the onion and spread over the fish, add a bay leaf and peppercorns. Cover the casserole and bake in a medium oven for about ½ hour or till the flesh is tender. Leave in the stock till cold. Serve the fish cut in thin slices across the grain or flaked, with mayonnaise flavoured with capers or serve with cocount

Coconut creamed fish

cream sauce (miti). Garnish with lemon slices and dill or parsley.
Serves 5-6

FISH CURRY

2 tablespoons butter
1 medium onion
1 clove garlic
1 tablespoon curry powder
3 peeled chopped, or ¾ cup canned tomatoes
1 tablespoon tomato paste or 2 tablespoons tomato puree
water
salt to taste
2 tablespoons lemon juice
750 gms (1½ lbs) fish fillet

Saute finely chopped onion and crushed garlic in butter for a few minutes. Add curry powder. Stir well, reduce heat and cook for a few minutes. Add tomato paste and tomatoes. Stir well, add a little water to make a thick sauce. Season with salt and add lemon juice. Place fish fillets in the sauce and simmer till cooked
Serves 6

COCONUT CREAMED FISH

750 gms (1½ lb) fish fillets
2 cups coconut cream
2 tablespoons chopped onion
1 teaspoon salt
chilli
1 tablespoon cornflour
oil
tomato
seasoned flour

Cut fish into servings. Pour coconut cream into a saucepan. add finely chopped onion, salt, chilli, (can be omitted) and cornflour, mixed to a paste with part of the cream. Bring to boiling point stirring all the time. Do not boil, but keep at simmering point for a few minutes. Dip fish in seasoned flour then fry till brown in hot oil. Drain well. Place fish in a casserole, pour over the sauce, put slices of tomato on top of fish, cover and bake at 150ºC (300ºF) for about 20 minutes. Serve with lemon wedges.
Serves 6

Baked ginger fish

BAKED GINGER FISH

Perfect for a dinner party. Looks and tastes superb.

1½ kg (2-3 lb) whole fish (schnapper, grouper or cod type)
1 lemon
2 teaspoons crushed green ginger
1 clove crushed garlic
¼ cup of soy sauce
½ cup oil
¾ cup of white wine or water
2 teaspoons sugar
chopped parsley, coriander or finely sliced green ginger

Clean fish and remove scales. Leave the head and tail intact. Dry well, and then rub with lemon juice. Leave for an hour or so in the refrigerator.

Combine crushed ginger, garlic, soy sauce and half the oil, water or wine. Mix thoroughly, This is best carried out in the blender. Rub the fish with the remaining oil. Place fish in a flat dish and pour over the ginger mixture. Bake in moderate oven and baste frequently with pan sauce till tender — about ½ an hour. Sprinkle with sugar and turn up heat, or put under the griller for a few minutes to melt the sugar and form a glaze. Serve the fish on a flat plate with pan sauce in a jug or bowl. Garnish with the sliced ginger and chopped parsley or coriander.

Note: It may be necessary to add extra wine or water to the pan sauce.

Variation
Add ½ cup of thick coconut cream to the sauce.
Serves 6
(Pacific Islands Cookbook)

FISH IN LEAVES

Using spinach, taro or beet leaves.

750 gms (1½ lb) fish fillets
12 spinach, taro or beet leaves
1 large onion
salt
2 cups coconut cream
4-6 tomatoes

Cut fillets into servings about 5-8cm (2-3 ins) long and 4 cm (1½ in) thick. Remove the stalks from 12 taro or beet leaves. Soften the beet leaves by slicing off half the back leaf rib and then soaking in hot water till pliable. Place 2 leaves together making sure that any holes are overlapped and the top side is up. Place the fish in the middle, sprinkle with chopped onion and a little salt. Hold each leaf parcel in the cup of your hand and pour in a little coconut cream. Fold over the leaves to make a parcel and secure with a toothpick. Place in a casserole and pour over remaining coconut cream. Put a slice of tomato on top of each parcel, cover and bake in a moderate oven for 30 minutes or till leaves are tender. Remove the toothpicks before serving.
Serves 6

FISH PUFF

½ kg (1 lb) white fish fillets
2 cups flour
1 teaspoon salt
6 oz (175 gm) margarine or butter
water
2 oz (60 gm) butter
1 tablespoon chopped parsley
salt and pepper
1 egg yolk

Cut fish into thin fillets. Prepare flaky pastry as follows. Make plain short pastry using flour, salt, margarine and cold water. Roll out to 1 cm (½ in) thickness. Dot butter on top half of pastry, fold up bottom and turn in sides. Repeat folding and rolling 3 more times. Chill for half an hour before using. Roll out pastry till 24 cm (10 in) wide and 30 cm (12 in) long. Place fillets in the middle leaving about 4 cm (1½ in) at each end and sufficient pastry at the sides to fold over and meet in the middle. Mix the butter with chopped parsley and put in dots on top of fish. Season with salt and pepper. Fold over sides and ends and pinch together. Brush the top with beaten egg yolk. Bake in hot oven for 15 minutes then at moderate heat for 15-20 minutes till golden brown and crisp. Serve hot or cold with lemon wedges and a salad.
Serves 6

CRAB VAKASOSO

A delicious buffet dish cooked in a coconut shell or casserole. Ideal for a buffet dinner. Fish or prawns may also be substituted for crab.

1 large crab
(2 cups cooked crab, fish or prawns)
1 bunch Chinese cabbage
1 medium onion
1 medium tomato
1 whole or 2 small coconuts, grated
⅓ cup thick coconut cream

Boil and remove meat from crab or cook enough fish to yield 2 cups. Finely shred Chinese cabbage and blanch in boiling salted water for about 2 minutes. Strain and put aside.
Grate the onion and finely chop the tomato. Take the whole mature coconut, carefully saw the top off it to make a lid (the end with the 'eyes') and grate some of the flesh out with a knife or coconut grater, leaving a thin coating inside.
Mix crab, tomato, onion, cabbage and 2 tablespoons grated coconut together, place it all in the shell and pour ⅓ cup of thick coconut cream over the top. Place the lid of the coconut back on top and put in a saucepan with some water to steam for 10-15 minutes. Serve in the shell and accompany with rice and salad. Alternatively, put mixture in a covered casserole and bake in oven for 15 to 20 minutes.
Serves 4

Crab vakasoso

FIJI CRAB

**1 medium crab 500 gms (1 lb)
or two 250 gm crabs
water
1 medium sized onion
1 clove garlic
2 tablespoons oil
1 large tomato
¼ teaspoon salt
pepper
2 beaten eggs**

Cook the crab in boiling water till it changes colour. Cool and remove the claws and legs. Take the flesh out of the back, claws and legs but keep the shell for final part of preparation. Chop the onion and garlic and fry in hot oil till golden. Mix with finely chopped tomato, crab meat and well beaten eggs. Season with salt and pepper. Put the mixture in the crab shell and bake in a medium oven till the egg sets, about 10-15 minutes. The crab mixture may also be baked in ramekins or small ovenware dishes for individual servings.
Serves 4

CRAYFISH with ZUCCHINI

Zucchini may be substituted with duruka, a delicious tropical vegetable becoming widely available.

**500 gms (1 lb) cooked crayfish
8 small zucchini or duruka
½ cup finely chopped onion
¼ cup chopped capsicums
4 tablespoons butter
1 cup milk, or coconut cream
2 teaspoons lemon juice
½ cup flour
2 cups vegetable stock
salt and pepper**

Slice zucchini or peel duruka and simmer in 2 cups salted water for 10 minutes. Strain into bowl and save the liquid. Heat butter and saute chopped onion and capsicum. Add crayfish and stir-fry with onion and capsicum for 5 minutes. Mix milk or coconut cream with flour till a smooth mix-

Tropical dressed crab

ture is formed and add lemon juice. Add liquid saved from cooking zucchini or duruka to the flour mixture and simmer till thick. Cut zucchini into 3-4 cm pieces. Now combine crayfish mixture and zucchini or duruka and fold in the sauce. Serve with rice, potato or similar.
Serves 6 to 8

PRAWN & FISH SCALLOP

**½ clove garlic
1 tablespoon onion
3 tablespoons butter
3 tablespoons flour
½ cup fish stock
½ cup tomato puree
salt, pepper
2 tablespoons sherry
1 cup milk
½ cup grated cheese
1 cup of cooked, shelled prawns
1 cup cooked flaked fish
1½ cups cooked rice
½ cup grated cheese
4 tomatoes**

Saute chopped onion and crushed garlic in butter. Stir in flour. Gradually stir in fish stock, tomato puree, salt and pepper and milk. Bring to the boil stirring all the time. Now add sherry, grated cheese, prawns (save a few to decorate the top), fish and rice.
Place the mixture in a greased baking dish or individual dishes. Cut the prawns in half lengthwise. Peel and slice tomatoes and arrange alternate

prawns and tomato slices on the top. Sprinkle with grated cheese and then bake in moderate oven till golden brown.

Variation
2 tablespoons chopped celery or 2 tablespoons chopped capsicums added to sauce.
Serves 6

TROPICAL DRESSED CRAB

A colorful and tasty way of serving crab.

**1½ cups cooked and flaked crab meat
1 head and claws of large crab
½ cup finely diced celery
½ cup finely diced cucumber
2 teaspoons lemon juice
salt and pepper to taste
½ cup coconut cream sauce
(see page 24)
or ½ cup mayonnaise
chopped dill or parsley**

Put the flaked crab in a bowl, add celery and cucumber, sprinkle with lemon juice, salt and pepper and toss well. Now fold in the coconut cream sauce or mayonnaise. Arrange the crab attractively on a large platter, using the head and claws and colourful vegetables to decorate the dish. Garnish the crab with a little chopped dill or parsley.

Lamb and Mutton

The quality of lamb or mutton can vary. Always enquire whether it is first or second grade. Generally, second grade meat contains more fat, and in the case of mutton, the sheep is older. Second grade meat needs careful cooking. To ensure tender meat, cook for a longer time at a lower temperature. Marinades are another excellent means of tenderising lamb and mutton and they also add flavour. Use rosemary, mint, thyme, sage, turmeric, cardamom, lemon, soy sauce, ginger or tomato to add richness and variety to lamb and mutton.

Marinades for Lamb & Mutton

sufficient for 750 gm (1½ lb) meat

¼ cup lemon juice or wine
¼ cup salad oil
½ teaspoon salt
½ teaspoon pepper
clove crushed garlic
or
2 tablespoons soy sauce
¼ cup salad oil
2 teaspoons chopped onion
1 teaspoon crushed green ginger

MARINATED LAMB CHOPS

As with any marinade, the longer the meat is left in the better the flavour.

1 kg (2 lb) lamb mid-loin chops
¼ cup oil
1 clove garlic
1 tablespoon chopped parsley
1 teaspoon chopped basil
freshly ground black pepper
salt to taste
2 tablespoons prepared French mustard

1 tablespoon anchovy sauce
2 tablespoons lemon juice

Trim any excess fat off chops. Mix oil with ½ clove crushed garlic and black pepper, parsley, basil and salt. Cover chops with marinade and leave for 4-5 hours.
Mix French mustard with anchovy sauce, lemon juice, ground black pepper and ½ clove crushed garlic. Spread ½ the mixture on the chops, then grill. When brown, turn over and spread with remaining mixture and grill till well browned. Alternatively, spread mixture on both sides of the chops, arrange in baking pan uncovered and cook in oven at 180°C (350°F) for 1 hour or until cooked.
Serves 4-6

BAKED LAMB EASTERN STYLE

2½ kg (5 lb) leg of lamb
1 medium onion

1 clove garlic
2 cm (1 in) piece of green ginger
¼ cup oil
1 tablespoon sesame oil
1 tablespoon soy sauce
½ teaspoon ground black pepper
stock or water
cornflour

Trim excess fat from leg of lamb and place in a baking pan. Score the skin with the tip of a sharp knife. Mince, or puree in a blender, the onion, garlic, and ginger. Add oil, sesame oil, soy sauce and pepper. Pour the mixture over the lamb and place in a moderate oven for 2½ hours. Baste several times during the cooking. Take the lamb out of the pan and keep hot. Skim fat off the top of the drippings and add water or stock to make sufficient gravy. Measure liquid and add 2 teaspoons of cornflour, mixed with a little water, to each cup of liquid. Bring to the boil stirring all the time. Serve lamb with the hot gravy.
Serves 6

Baked lamb eastern style

BANANA LAMB CASSEROLE

A recipe that has its origins in equatorial Africa.

**3 cups sliced green bananas
(about 6 bananas, plantain or cooking bananas are best)
water
1 medium onion
2 medium tomatoes
1 large capsicum
2 tablespoons oil
1 kg (1 lb) lean lamb shoulder
(minced or cut into small cubes)
1 cup water
2 tablespoons peanut butter
½ teaspoon chilli sauce
(optional)
salt and pepper to taste**

Peel the bananas and slice. Cover with water and leave 1 to 2 hours.

Chop the onion, tomatoes and the capsicum. Heat oil and saute lamb till brown. Remove lamb, saute the onion and then add capsicum and tomatoes. Combine with lamb and cook together for 5 minutes, stirring well. Now add the banana and cook for a further 5 minutes. Mix water, peanut butter and chilli together till smooth and pour over meat and simmer till almost dry. Put into a casserole and bake in a medium oven for 10 minutes. Serve with rice or root vegetables and a salad.
Serves 5-6

MUTTON or LAMB KORMA

A medium spicy dish using yoghurt.

**1 kg (2 lb) mutton or lamb cutlets
1 clove garlic
1 teaspoon crushed green ginger
½ cup yoghurt
1 large onion**

**6 cloves
4 cardamom pods
4 cm (1½ in) stick of cinnamon
4 tablespoons oil or ghee
½ cup of yoghurt
1 teaspoon salt
1 cup coconut cream or yoghurt**

Trim fat off chops. Crush the garlic and combine with ginger and ½ cup yoghurt and brush mixture over chops. Leave several hours. Finely slice large onion, bruise the cloves, cardamom pods and cinnamon stick with a rolling pin. Heat oil or ghee and saute onion and then add spices. Cook 4-5 minutes till onion is soft but not brown. Add the meat, ½ cup coconut cream or yoghurt and salt. Cover with lid and simmer till meat is cooked. If desired, add coconut cream or extra yoghurt before serving. Serve with rice.
Serves 6

COCONUT LAMB SHOULDER CASSEROLE

A very special and exciting way to cook lamb

2 large onions
¼ cup oil
1 kg (2 lb) boned lamb shoulder
½ cup white wine
½ cup tomato puree
½ cup water
2 tablespoons cornflour
¼ cup water
1 teaspoon salt
freshly ground black pepper
½ teaspoon dried marjoram
1 cup sour cream or yoghurt
1 cup grated coconut

Peel onions and cut into cubes. Fry in hot oil till golden. Cut lamb into cubes, removing fat, and add to onion. Saute for a few minutes. Add wine, tomato puree and water. Simmer for 1 hour or till tender. Mix cornflour with water and stir into the lamb. Season with salt, pepper and marjoram. Stir in sour cream or yoghurt just before serving. Put in a serving dish and top with grated coconut. Put under the griller and lightly brown coconut. Serve with mashed potato or noodles.
Serves 6

MADRAS MUTTON CURRY

750 gms (1½ lb) lean mutton
4 tablespoons oil or ghee
1 clove garlic
1 medium onion
1 tablespoon curry powder
1 tablespoon tomato paste
(or 3-4 fresh, peeled tomatoes)
1 teaspoon salt
2 teaspoons lemon juice

Cut mutton into cubes. Heat oil or ghee in a saucepan and add crushed garlic and finely chopped onion. Saute until onion starts to colour. Add curry powder. Stir well and saute a few minutes. Add meat and tomato paste, or chopped tomatoes, salt and lemon juice. Stir well and simmer on low heat till meat is tender. Extra stock or water may be added if more gravy is needed. Serve with rice.
Serves 6
Note: For a stronger curry flavour add an extra tablespoon of curry powder.

CINNAMON MANGO CHOPS

loin chops
salt
pepper
mango slices
melted butter
cinnamon

Season loin chops (two for each person if small, one if large) with pepper and salt and then grill. Just before chops are cooked, remove from the grill and place thin slices of mango on each chop, brush with melted butter, sprinkle with cinnamon and return to the grill. Cook until the mango is tender and slightly brown. Serve hot with sweet potato baked in the skin and a green vegetable.

Variation
Substitute ripe peach for mango.

Cinnamon mango chops

36

Barbecued lamb shanks

BARBECUED LAMB SHANKS

2 kg (4 lb) lamb shanks
½ cup seasoned flour
2 tablespoons oil
1 cup sliced onion
1 cup tomato sauce
1 cup water
1 teaspoon salt
1 teaspoon garlic salt
1 teaspoon onion salt
**2 tablespoons Worcestershire
sauce**
¼ cup vinegar
¼ cup sugar
2 teaspoons dry mustard
1 teaspoon paprika

Cover lamb shanks in seasoned flour and fry in hot oil until golden. Place in a large casserole dish. Cover and bake in 190ºC (375ºF) oven for 1 hour. Remove from oven and drain off excess fat. Prepare barbecue sauce with sliced onion, tomato sauce, water, salt, garlic salt, onion salt, Worcestershire sauce, vinegar, sugar, dry mustard and paprika. Pour half the sauce over lamb, cover and return to oven. Bake further ½ hour. Remove cover and baste with remaining sauce every 10 minutes for the next hour. Serve with boiled rice and salads.
Serves 8

KOFTA CURRY

Meat balls with a creamy, curry sauce

1 clove garlic
1 small onion
500 gms (1 lb) minced lamb or beef
¼ teaspoon black pepper
¼ teaspoon ground cloves
¼ teaspoon ground cinnamon
1 egg
½ cup oil or ghee
1 large onion

1 teaspoon turmeric
1 teaspoon ground coriander
½ teaspoon ground ginger
a dash chilli powder
2 cups coconut cream
½ teaspoon salt
2 teaspoons lemon juice
1½ cups rice

Mince garlic and onion and combine with finely minced meat. Add pepper, cinnamon, cloves and beaten egg and mix thoroughly. Form into balls with floured hands. Fry in hot butter or ghee, till brown and remove from pan.
Chop large onion finely and fry in remaining fat till golden. Add all remaining spices and saute 3-4 minutes. Pour coconut cream over spices and onion and add salt and lemon juice. Now return meat balls to the saucepan and simmer for 30 minutes.
Serves 6

COCONUT MINT RACK OF LAMB

2 kg (4 lb) rack of lamb
½ cup of water
oil
1 cup grated coconut
½ cup fine dry breadcrumbs
2 tablespoons chopped mint
1 tablespoon water
salt
pepper
coconut cream

Roast the rack of lamb by placing it in a baking dish, with half a cup of water. Brush with oil and bake at 180ºC (350ºF). Mix coconut, dry breadcrumbs, mint, water and seasoning together. About 15 minutes before the lamb is cooked, remove from the oven and sprinkle with the coconut mixture. Press down with a spatula or spoon and return to oven before serving. Add a little coconut cream to the gravy just before serving. Serve lamb with guava jelly.
Serves 6

LAMB & EGGPLANT CASEROLE

A good way of using cooked lamb or mutton

300 gms (12 oz) cooked lamb
1 medium onion finely chopped
1 clove garlic, crushed
150 gms (6 oz) eggplant peeled
¼ cup butter
3 tablespoons flour
1½ cups well seasoned stock
1 cup rich milk
1 bay leaf
½ teaspoon rosemary
salt and pepper
½ cup soft breadcrumbs
1 teaspoon butter

Cut lamb into small cubes. slice onion and finely chop garlic. Saute onion and garlic in butter. Slice the eggplant and combine with onion and garlic and saute until golden brown, adding extra butter if necessary. Take out egglant, onion and garlic leaving the remaining juices.
Using pan juices, prepare a sauce by adding the flour, stock and milk, stirring constantly, Season with bay leaf and rosemary. Simmer for 5 minutes. Place alternate layers of lamb, onion and eggplant in a casserole and pour over the sauce. Sprinkle with soft breadcrumbs mixed with 1 tablespoon of melted butter. Bake in 180ºC (350ºF) oven for 30 minutes or until brown on top.

Coconut mint rack of lamb

Veal

Good veal should have a pale colour and a fine texture. Like other meats it must be properly matured to make it tender.

Darker coloured veal comes from the more mature animals. To make this tender pound well and use the marinades as given on page 41 under Beef.

Veal has a delicate flavour which can be enhanced with the addition of lemon, white wine, parsley, sage, thyme, oregano, onion, garlic tomato, sour cream, yoghurt and cheese.

Veal is best served with rich, delicately flavoured sauces and stuffings.

Mushroom veal

MUSHROOM VEAL

1 kg (2 lb) veal steak or fillet
½ cup flour
1 teaspoon salt
¼ teaspoon pepper
2 tablespoons butter
2 tablespoons oil
3 cloves garlic
2 cups chicken stock
2 tablespoons cornflour
½ cup dry white wine
2 tablespoons tomato paste
4 medium onions
3 medium tomatoes
1 cup sliced mushrooms
¼ cup chopped parsley

Cut veal into 4 cm cubes (1½ in). Combine with flour, salt and pepper. Heat butter and oil and brown veal. Remove and drain. Finely chop garlic and fry till golden, adding extra oil if needed. Mix cornflour with chicken stock and stir into pan. When smooth add wine and tomato paste. Simmer for a minute. Place veal in casserole, pour over sauce. Cut onions into quarters and arrange on top. Cover with lid and bake at 160ºC (325ºF) for one hour. Peel tomatoes and cut into eighths. Put on top of veal together with mushrooms. Cover and bake another 20 minutes. Just before serving stir chopped parsley into the casserole. Serve with green vegetables and rice, noodles or mashed potato.
Serves 6-8

VEAL WITH TUNA SAUCE

An ideal summer dish served cold, garnished with chopped parsley and accompanied with salad

1½ kg (3 lbs) piece of veal
½ cup lemon juice
2 cups water
1 tablespoons anchovy sauce
1 teaspoon salt
½ teaspoon pepper
2 bayleaves
½ sliced onion
2 cloves
175 gms (6 oz) cooked or canned tuna
1½ tablespoons anchovy sauce
1 tablespoon chopped capers
2 tablespoons lemon juice
½ teaspoon pepper freshly ground
½ teaspoon salt
½ cup mayonnaise

Tie veal together with a string and place in a casserole. Combine lemon juice, water, anchovy sauce, salt and pepper; pour over meat. Add bay leaf, sliced onion and cloves. Cover and bake 2-2½ hours at 150ºC (300ºF) and leave in stock until cold. Prepare sauce by finely mashing tuna with a fork and combining with anchovy sauce, chopped capers, lemon juice, freshly ground black pepper, salt and mayonnaise. Take veal out of stock, remove string and pour over sauce. Refrigerate overnight.
Serve sliced covered with sauce and garnished with parsley and olives.
Serves 6

VEAL ROUROU

Using spinach, taro or beet leaves

4 veal steaks
⅔ cup cooked chopped taro or beet leaves
4 slices Cheddar cheese
½ cup seasoned flour
1 beaten egg
1 tablespoon water
2 tablespoons butter
2 tablespoons oil
½ cup breadcrumbs

Veal with tuna sauce

Prepare veal steaks by pounding until thin. Place 2 tablespoons cooked chopped spinach (taro or beet leaves) on each slice of veal, followed by a thin slice of Cheddar cheese. Fold in half and secure with a toothpick. Dip veal in seasoned flour then in beaten egg to which water has been added. Press breadcrumbs onto veal, chill for 1-2 hours. Fry in a moderately hot pan with butter and oil, cooking for 5-7 minutes on each side. Serve immediately.
Serves 4

TROPICAL VEAL BIRDS

An unusual and exciting recipe using fermented coconut (Kora) or yoghurt to give a piquant flavour.

750 gms (1½ lb) veal steak
185 gm (6 oz) minced veal
1 small onion
½ cup breadcrumbs
1 beaten egg
¼ teaspoon rosemary
½ teaspoon salt
¼ teaspoon freshly ground pepper
1 clove garlic
½ cup seasoned flour
3 tablespoons butter
1 cup chicken stock
½ cup cream
1 tablespoon thick plain yoghurt or Kora (see page 10)

Pound veal steak. Cut into pieces 5-10 cm (2-4 in). Mix minced veal with onion, breadcrumbs, beaten egg, rosemary, salt, and freshly ground black pepper to make stuffing. Rub veal steaks with clove of garlic. Place 1 tablespoon of stuffing on each piece of veal, roll and fasten with a toothpick. Cover with seasoned flour and brown in hot butter in frying pan. Add chicken stock, cover and simmer for 1 hour. Remove veal to a serving plate and keep hot. Stir cream and yoghurt or Kora into pan juices. Add a little water if too much of the pan juices have evaporated. Cover veal with sauce and serve with slices of lemon.
Serves 6

Beef

Good quality beef is often sold before it has properly matured. Beef must hang for 3-4 days at about 10°C (60°F) to enable the tenderising process to take place.

Fresh beef should be kept in the bottom of the refrigerator, loosely covered, for 3-4 days before using. Remove any liquid that forms and turn over daily.

To develop the flavour of beef, use any of these spices and herbs - ginger, garlic, marjoram, basil, bayleaf, cinnamon, clove, cumin, nutmeg, mace, mustard, sage, thyme, soy sauce, and tamarind.

Beef can be made more tender by marinating for 4-5 hours in one of these mixtures. (Sufficient for about 750 gms (1½ lb of meat)

1. ¼ cup lemon juice, ¼ cup salad oil, ½ teaspoon salt, ½ teaspoon pepper, ½ crushed clove garlic, or replace lemon juice with wine.

2. 2 tablespoons soy sauce, ¼ cup salad oil, 2 teaspoons chopped onion, 1 teaspoon crushed green ginger.

3. Cook tough steak at a low temperature 120°C (275°F) with plenty of tomato, or other acidic fruit, or use chopped green or ripe pawpaw, pineapple or kiwifruit.

KEBABS

Delicious kebabs can be made out of any tender meat combined with a variety of vegetables. Fun to make and eat. To make kebabs, cut meat into 2 cm (1 inch) cubes. Meat may be marinated in a flavoured sauce.

Thread alternate pieces of meat, sliced onion, green peppers, eggplant, mushrooms and tomato on a skewer. Brush with oil or melted butter. Season well. Grill slowly over a barbecue or hot coals or under an electric griller.

Kebabs should be served with rice, and preferably a good rich sauce made from wine, tomato, soy sauce and ginger or peanuts.

Kebabs

SPICED CORNED BEEF

This recipe provides an excellent main course for lunches, suppers and buffet meals. Silverside is leaner than brisket. If meat is very salty, soak for several hours in cold water before cooking. Cook, well-covered in water.

1½ kg (3 lb) corned beef
1 teaspoon turmeric
½ teaspoon cayenne pepper
water
4-5 peppercorns
½ cup vinegar
¼ cup sugar
3-4 cloves
1 bay leaf

Weigh and allow 35-40 minutes of cooking time per 500 gms (1 lb) meat. Thoroughly dry raw corned silverside with a paper towel. Combine turmeric and cayenne pepper. Rub it onto outside of meat. Place in a large saucepan and cover with water. Season with peppercorns, vinegar, sugar, cloves and the bay leaf. Bring to boil, reduce heat and simmer gently for remaining time. Remove from water. Wrap in foil to keep moist and continue to cool slowly.
Serves 6-8

ORANGE GLAZED CORNED BEEF

Spiced corned beef marmalade

Prepare spiced corned beef as in previous recipe. Remove from saucepan 20 minutes before cooking time. Spread thickly with about ½ cup marmalade and bake in oven for 20 minutes at 180°C (350°F)

Pineapple glazed corned beef
A delicious variation of the orange glaze. Use drained, crushed pineapple and sugar in place of marmalade. Bake as directed above.

EGGPLANT STEAK

4 fillet or sirloin steaks
1 tablespoon French mustard
2 tablespoons oil
4 slices eggplant, 1 cm thick
¼ cup milk
¼ cup seasoned flour
2 tablespoons oil
2 tablespoons parsley butter

Spread steaks with French mustard, and pan fry in hot oil. Dip eggplant in milk and then in seasoned flour. Fry until crisp and then drain on brown paper. Serve steak on slices of eggplant. Garnish with parsley butter.
Serves 4

Parsley Butter
Beat 120 gm (4 oz) butter till soft and add 2 teaspoons finely chopped parsley.

Right: Eggplant steak

Orange glazed corned beef

PALUSAMI

Palusami is a traditional Samoan dish made from taro leaves, coconut cream and a variety of fillings. Silver-beet leaves make a good substitute for taro leaves. The usual filling for Palusami is corned beef and onion, but seafoods like prawns and fish are also delicious. Palusami may be prepared for individual servings or as a main dish.

**24-34 young taro leaves
(or silverbeet leaves)
1 cup coconut cream
250 gm (8oz) cooked corned beef
1 medium onion
2 medium tomatoes
1 cup thick coconut cream
salt to taste**

Cut out the central stalk from leaves. Cut onion and tomato into thin slices. For individual servings, arrange 4-5 leaves overlapping one another. Ensure that the underside of the leaf is on top and all the holes are covered.

Arrange leaves in order of size so that larger ones are underneath and smaller leaves inside. For individual servings hold leaves in the palm of the hand to form a cup. For larger servings place leaves on a flat surface. In both cases put the first measure of coconut cream and beef in the centre of the leaves, add a layer of onion and tomato, season with salt and slowly pour in 1 cup of thick coconut cream, lifting the edge of the leaves to prevent this escaping. Fold over the leaves to make a neat parcel. Secure the ends with with a toothpick or tie up with cotton or banana fibre. Wrap in foil or wilted banana leaf, put it in a covered container and bake in a moderate oven 30-40 minutes or longer for a large parcel. Alternatively, cook in a steamer. Serve hot or cold.

Serves 6

Leaves overlap to form a package for ingredients

Palusami tied up ready to bake or steam

Palusami

44

MEAT BALLS with SWEET & SOUR SAUCE

750 gms (1½ lb) fine minced beef
1 medium onion minced
2 eggs
¼ teaspoon pepper
¼ teaspoon grated nutmeg
1 teaspoon salt
1 clove garlic crushed
2 tablespoons oil

Use fine, or twice minced meat, and combine with minced onion. Blend in egg, pepper, nutmeg, salt, and crushed clove of garlic. Form into small balls and chill for at least 1 hour. Fry balls in oil until brown, and cooked through. Drain and keep warm.

Sauce

¾ cup sugar
1 cup vinegar
1 cup water
1 small clove crushed garlic
½ teaspoon crushed green ginger
1 tablespoon cornflour
1 teaspoon salt
¼ cup water
1 cup chopped capsicums
2 cups cubed pineapple
or pawpaw

Combine sugar, vinegar, water, crushed green ginger and crushed garlic. Bring to boil. Stir in salt and cornflour which has been mixed to a paste with water. Simmer until thick. Finally, add chopped capsicum, cubed pineapple, or pawpaw and then meat balls. Simmer for 5 minutes and serve with rice or noodles.
Serves 6

STEAK & PINEAPPLE

1 steak per person (fillet, rump, etc)
salt
freshly ground black pepper
pineapple rings
oil

Season steak with salt and pepper. Pan fry in oil or grill. Serve with slices of lightly fried pineapple.

Meat balls with sweet and sour sauce

SATE with PEANUT SAUCE

A famous Indonesian dish, traditionally served with rice.

750 gm (1½ lb) beef
(chicken or pork may be used)
1 cup coconut cream
2 teaspoons soy sauce
1 tablespoon sugar
1 tablespoon lemon juice
2 cloves crushed garlic
1 small onion finely chopped
salt to taste

Cut meat into 2 cm (½ in) cubes. Prepare a marinade of coconut cream, soy sauce, sugar, lemon juice, crushed cloves of garlic, finely chopped onion and a little salt. Marinate meat for several hours, thread the cubes onto skewers and grill over charcoal or under an electric or gas griller until cooked. Serve with peanut sauce

Peanut Sauce

1 onion
1 teaspoon chopped green ginger
2 cloves garlic
2 tablespoons peanut oil
4 tablespoons peanut butter
2 cups coconut cream
2 tablespoons soy sauce
2 teaspoons sugar
1 chilli
1 tablespoon lemon juice
salt to taste

Chop onion finely, crush ginger and garlic and saute altogether in hot oil. Add peanut butter and coconut cream. Mix, or blend well. Now add soy sauce, sugar, chopped seeded chilli, lemon juice and salt. Stir well and simmer for 5 minutes. Makes 2½ cups

BEEF CURRY

This never-fail curry has an excellent flavour. Extra vegetables such as beans, carrots, and eggplant may be added as an option. Serve this curry with rice and accompaniments.

1 medium onion
2-3 chillies
¼ cup oil
1 teaspoon cumin seed
2 tablespoons curry powder
1 teaspoon turmeric
500 gm (1 lb) blade steak
1 teaspoon salt
2 cm (1 in) piece green ginger
4 cloves garlic
1 medium tomato
1 cup cubed raw potato

Finely chop onion and chillies. Saute in oil with cumin seed until onion is golden. Add the curry powder and turmeric and then the cubed blade steak. Cover and cook for 10 minutes stirring occasionally. Mash garlic and ginger with the salt. Add to curry, cover and cook for 5 minutes more. Stir in chopped tomatoes and cubed raw potatoes. Any other vegetables should be added at this point. Simmer until potato is soft.
Serves 4

BEEF KOVU

Beef cooked in a parcel. A good recipe for less tender cuts of beef.

750 gm (1½ lb) stewing steak
2 medium sized onions
2 cups sweet potato or cooking bananas
3-4 tomatoes
2 cups coconut cream
1 teaspoon salt
foil, or banana leaves

At left: Beef curry

At right: Beef kovu

Cut stewing steak into cubes, slice onions, sweet potatoes or cooking bananas, and tomatoes. Prepare coconut cream (also available in cans). Combine all ingredients and sprinkle with salt. Wrap in foil or wilted banana leaves (see section on Essentials of Tropical Cooking). Tie up and cook in a steamer for 2-2½ hours. Alternatively, place in covered casserole with a little water and cook in moderate oven for 2-2½ hours.
Serves 4

Pork

Pork may be prepared in numerous ways. It is equally good roasted, boiled, or cut into fine shreds and sauteed with vegetables. Because of its bland flavour, the choice of flavourings is important.

Use cardamom, allspice, celery, ginger, sage, clove, coriander and fennel. Soy sauce, orange, apple and pineapple also go well with pork. Fresh pork or ham may be glazed with honey, golden syrup or brown sugar.

ROAST HONEY PORK

2-2½ kg (4-5 lb) leg of pork
1 tablespoon green ginger
2 tablespoons oil
2 teaspoons ginger
2 teaspoons salt
½ cup honey

Score leg of pork by cutting through the skin and fat in a criss-cross fashion. Run a knife between the skin and the meat to form a pocket. Grate green ginger and spread evenly into pocket. Mix oil, ground ginger and salt together, brush over pork and place in oven at 180°C (350°F). Periodically brush with remaining oil while cooking. Allow 60 minutes of cooking time per kilo. Glaze pork by pouring honey over it about 15 minutes before it is done. Delicious with candied carrots and sweet potato, taro or cassava cakes.

Variation
Pineapple juice may be used in place of honey.

ROAST PORK LEG

4-5 kg (8-10 lb) leg
water

dried ground cloves
salt

Ask the butcher to score the skin with the point of a sharp knife at ¼ inch intervals in the leg of pork. Pour a jug full of boiling water over the leg. When dry, rub with a sprinkling of dried cloves and salt. Put the pork in an oven at 260°C (500°F) and cook for an hour till outside is golden and crisp. Reduce heat to 150°C (300°F) and cook for another 2-2½ hours or until done. (About 60 mins per kilo)

PORK IN SOUR CREAM

A rich and tangy dish which is easy to prepare.

750 gm (1½ lb) pork chops or steak
½ cup seasoned flour
½ cup oil
½ cup sour cream or yoghurt
2 tablespoons lemon juice
1 teaspoon salt
1 teaspoon dried thyme
1 teaspoon sugar
water
chopped parsley

Trim excess fat off meat and cut into servings. Season flour with salt and pepper, roll meat in flour and then brown in hot oil. Place in casserole. Mix sour cream, lemon juice, salt, thyme and sugar together and pour over the meat. Add sufficient water to cover meat. Cover casserole and bake at 180°C (350°F) for one hour or till tender. Garnish with chopped parsley and serve with sweet potato and mixed green salad.
Serves 5-6

Pork in sour cream

Taste of the Tropics

The Complete guide to tropical fruit & vegetables

41 full colour pictures. Information on selection, uses, storage and nutrition

Introduction

Modern transport now takes tropical fruits and vegetables to every part of the world. Exotic produce is to be found in supermarkets or fruit and vegetable shops in most large cities and towns.

The best quality produce is often found in shops which cater for people from tropical countries.

Sometimes there are shops which specialise in importing foods from the south Pacific, Africa or the West Indies. Here the quality of foods and the variety available are likely to be very good. There are also some supermarkets which specialise in tropical foods.

The Nutritive Value of Commonly Used Tropical Fruits and Vegetables

per 4 ounce (100 g) prepared raw food

	Calories	Protein	Fat	Carbohydrate	Calcium	Iron	Vit.A.	Thiamin	Vit.C.
	Number	g	g	g	mg	mg	mg	mg	mg
Vegetables									
Bitter Melon	19	0.8	0.1	4.5	26	2.3	110	0.06	57
Long beans	36	4	0.6	6	54	1.4	455	.14	24
Winged beans	25	2		5	63	0.6	63	0.21	
Chilies, Red	45	5	0.8	9	11	0.9	4770	0.09	15
Eggplant	26	2	0.3	6	22	0.9	50	0.08	86
Chinese cabbage	40	3	0.7	8	192	2.4	1200	0.04	40
Taro leaves	61	4	1	12	162	1	5535	0.13	63
Squash, white fleshed	17	0.7	0.1	4	25	0.5	30	0.03	6
Okra	31	1.8	0.1	7.6	90	1	140	0.07	18
Starchy Roots, Fruits									
Breadfruit	113	1.5	0.4	26	25	1		0.1	20
Sweet potato, white	114	1.5	0.3	26	25	1		0.1	30
Sweet potato, yellow							1600		
Manoic (Cassava)	153	0.7	0.2	37	25	1		0.07	30
Plantain	128	0.1	0.2	31	7	0.5	30	0.05	20
Taro	113	0.2	0	26	25	1		0.1	20
Yam	104	2	0.2	24	10	1.2	6	0.1	10
Fruits									
Avocado	165	1.5	15	6	10	1	60	0.07	15
Bananas	116	1	0.3	27	7	0.5	30	0.05	10
Carambola	28	0.3	0.4	7	8	1	160	0.05	38
Ripe coconut	414	4	40	15	14	2.2		0.04	4
Green coconut	106	1.4	3.6	6	6	1		0.03	5
Custard Apple	76	1.5	0.3	19	27	0.5	20	0.11	21
Durian	124	2.5	1.6	28.3	20	0.9	trace	0.27	37
Guava	58	1	0.4	13	15	1	60	0.05	200
Jack fruit	94	1.7	0.3	23.7	27	0.6	235	0.09	9
Langsat (Langsard)	55	0.9	0.1	14.2	12	0.9	0	0.08	2
Longan	71	1.0	1.4	15.6	23	0.4	0	0.03	56
Lychee (Litchi)	65	0.8	0.4	16.3	10	0.3	0	0.05	50
Mango	63	0.5		15	10	0.5	180	0.03	50
Mangosteen	57	0.5	0.3	14.7	10	0.5	0	0.03	4
Melon, water	23	0.4		5	5	0.3	9	0.02	5
Papaya	39	0.6		9	20	0.5	120	0.03	50
Passionfruit	92	2.3	2	16	10	1	6		20
Pineapple	57	0.4		14	20	0.5	30	0.08	30
Pomelo	39	0.7	0.3	9.5	27	0.5	30	0.05	53
Rambutan	64	1.0	0.1	16.5	20	1.9	0	trace	23
Rose apple	30	0.5	0.1	7.6	18	0.4	0	0.03	17
Sapodilla	76	0.4	0.7	19.1	27	0.6	25	trace	13
Soursop	93	1		22	25	0.5		.1	30
Tahitian Apple	46	0.2	0.1	12.4	56	0.3	205	0.05	36

Reference: *Food composition tables for use in the South Pacific,* South Pacific Commission, Noumea, New Caledonia, 1983.
Food composition tables for use in East Asia, Food and Agricultural Organisation of U.N., 1972

Before shopping for your tropical fruits and vegetables, make sure that you know something about the food that you wish to try in your menu. Know how to choose good-quality items and have an idea as to how you will cook and serve them. If in doubt about trying out your family on something new, buy small quantities and have a tasting session. Most people will agree that these new foods add an exciting difference to daily meals, but not all will necessarily be to everyone's taste.

Having decided on the foods you are going to buy, think how you will use them in your menu. Choose foods which will complement the main meat or fish dish. For example, if serving pork you might accompany this with sweet potatoes and Chinese cabbage, followed by a pineapple and pawpaw dessert. If fish is your choice, think of serving this with taro leaves cooked in coconut cream and some yam, garnish with pieces of fresh lime and have a tossed tomato salad. Follow this course with a crisp orange and banana pie.

This section of our book is designed to help you know about the foods which will make an exciting difference to your meals and at the same time improve the nutritional value of the menu.

Avocado

Tropical varieties have a green or purple skin. Fruits vary in size but some of the best flavored are about the size of an orange. A ripe fruit is soft inside, but feels firm when pressed gently with the fingers.

Store ripe fruit in a cool place or refrigerate. Keep hard fruits in a warm dark cupboard till soft. Sliced avocado may be dipped in lemon juice and frozen whole or as a purée. (Lemon juice prevents cut fruit from going brown.)

To use cut ripe fruit in half, remove stone and any brown tissue, score with the tip of a knife and season with salt, pepper, lemon juice or French dressing. Serve halves filled with seafood or other savory mixtures. Purée fresh and frozen fruit to make mayonnaise, soups, or ice cream. Avocado purée combines well with bananas and soursop to make desserts. Mash and season for sandwich fillings. Frozen fruit does not keep its shape and is best used as a purée.

Food value has a high fat content and is a fair source of vitamins.

Bananas

The best eating bananas are the Cavendish and the short Ladies' Fingers. Both types should be firm and yellow when eaten.

Store in a cool dry place, preferably hanging. Mature green bananas may be ripened by putting in a large bag and hanging in a warm place. Freeze ripe bananas whole to make a refreshing iced snack for children. Split bananas and dry in the sun. Make into jam.

To use peel or mash and eat as a dessert with cream. To prevent browning sprinkle with lemon juice. Use bananas in fruit desserts like ice cream, mousse, jelly, or as a pie filling. Use in milk shakes. Fry and serve with bacon. For savories, cut in sections, roll in bacon and grill.

Food value a carbohydrate food which also provides vitamin C and some minerals. Ripe mashed banana is easily digested and makes a good first food for infants.

Coconut

Mature nuts should have a brown fibrous shell and water inside. Green coconuts provide a refreshing drink.

Store coconuts on shelves in a dry place. Mature nuts will last for several weeks, and green nuts for about a week. Coconut cream, made from the squeezed flesh of mature nuts, freezes well.

To use tap the shell sharply with a heavy knife around the centre. This cracks the shell evenly. Save the water for making coconut cream, or to drink. Grate or cut the flesh out of the shells. Add a little water to cut flesh and grind in a food processor or add water to grated flesh, then put coconut mixture into cheesecloth and squeeze out the cream.

Toast grated coconut in the oven and use as a topping for desserts. Use freshly grated coconut in cakes, scones, bread, sweets, biscuits, vegetable curry, and to make chutney.

Food value a good source of fat and fibre plus some protein.

Cumquat (Kumquat)

This small citrus fruit is bright yellow to green in colour. It has a distinctive tart flavour. Cumquat trees bear several times a year and the fruits are valued for their many uses.

Store on racks in a cool place or in perforated plastic bags in the refrigerator. Fruits last in good condition for 3-5 days in open storage. Cumquats make good preserves, and the cooked fruit freezes well.

To use cumquats have a high pectin content and make good jams and marmalades. A few cumquats will greatly improve the flavour of an orange or grapefruit marmalade. Whole fruits make good sweet or acid pickles which go well with pork and ham. Cumquat juice makes a good addition to any fruit drink. The pure juice is very acid and may be used to make raw fish dishes in place of lemon juice.

Food value a good source of Vitamin C.

Custard Apple

This tropical fruit comes from South America and the West Indies and is widely grown in tropical countries. It is also known as sugar apple and bullock's heart. Large heart-shaped fruits hang from bushy trees. Fruits are a brownish red color and contain several large seeds which are interspersed in a cream-colored, sweet and slightly granular pulp.

Store on racks. Pick when mature but still firm. Separate pulp from the seeds and freeze.

To use peel the brown skin of soft ripe fruits. The fruit tends to fall into segments which are best eaten fresh. Pulp may be removed from seeds and used in ice creams and sorbets.

Food value a fair source of vitamin C.

Durian

Oval fruit weighing 2-3 kg (5-7 lbs) are borne on large trees. Each fruit is covered in sharp pointed spikes. When mature the fruit becomes soft and has an offensive smell. The soft sweet pulp which surrounds large seeds is highly relished by durian eaters.
Store on racks in a cool, airy location away from the house. The smell of ripening fruits is offensive to many people.
To use peel off the spikey skin and separate the soft white segments. These should be eaten fresh. Some people say the flavour resembles gorgonzola cheese. The large seeds are edible.
Food value a fair source of vitamin C. Also contains a little protein and fat.

Eggplant (Aubergine)

Fruits are many colors, ranging from white, pale green and pale mauve to dark purple. Size varies according to variety. For the paler colored varieties, choose small to medium fruits. Mature fruits may have a lot of seeds. The newer types of dark purple fruits have more flesh and fewer seeds. For all kinds, fruits should be firm, skin tender and the end soft.
Store on wire racks in a cool place or in a container in the refrigerator. Fruits keep fresh for several days. Cooked eggplant dishes freeze well.
To use eggplant, peel, slice or cube. Young fruits may be cooked with the skin on. Dip slices in flour or batter and fry, sauté and add to vegetable dishes.
Food value is low.

Guava

Choose firm fruit of a large size and greenish yellow color. Small fruits tend to have a higher proportion of seed pulp.
Store on wire racks in a cool place or in the refrigerator. Firm fruits keep for several days in cool weather. Lightly cooked prepared fruit may be frozen. Ripe fruit has a strong smell.
To use wash and eat as raw fruit. Peel, cut in half, scoop out seed pulp, slice shells and cook in a syrup for about five minutes. Flavor with lemon juice and serve as dessert or add to fruit salad. Boil the pulp and strain. Use the purée to make jam or include in ice cream and gelatin desserts. Make jelly from half-ripe fruit. Boil up skins and half-ripe fruit to make fruit juice. The flavor of guava is enhanced by adding a little lemon juice. A guava ketchup for meat is made by replacing the tomato with guava purée in tomato sauce recipes.
Food value one of the best sources of vitamin C. A good raw fruit for children.

Jack Fruit

This tree bears fruits weighing up to 70 lbs (28 kg), which hang from the trunk and branches. Fruits are a greenish yellow color. Fruits have tough skin with a rough surface. Green fruit has a firm flesh which exudes a sticky sap on cutting. When ripe, sweet segments may be pulled from the core.

Store on wire shelves till ready to use. Green fruits will keep for 1-2 weeks before ripening. Cut green fruits will ripen if put into a closed plastic bag.

To use the sticky sap from jack fruit makes preparation difficult. This problem can be reduced by oiling hands, knives and preparation surfaces. Green fruits are cut into cubes and steamed or sautéed with curry spices, onion and garlic before adding stock or water. Jack fruit has a mushroom-like flavor. It makes a delicious vegetable curry. The ripe segments may be used as a fresh fruit or included in raw fruit dishes.

Food value a fair source of carbohydrate, vitamins and minerals.

Kiwano

Also known as Horned or Jelly melon or African horned cucumber. When fully ripened kiwano is a golden orange color, the pulp turning dark green and sweetening in flavor. It has a subtle taste of banana and lime.

Store may be stored at room temperature. If picked when first yellow ripening appears, fruit will keep up to six months in good conditions.

To use slice into wedges or cut in half lengthwise and eat directly from the shell with a spoon, sweetening and chilling if preferred. The pulp may be squeezed into a bowl to use in desserts, with ice cream, seafood cocktails or in long drinks.

Limes

Generally small in size with a smooth, brilliant green skin and a special aroma. Some varieties are yellow in color.

Store on racks in a cool place. If carefully handled they will keep for at least 7-10 days. Freeze the fresh juice in ice trays and keep in bags.

To use squeeze and flavor sweet and savory dishes. Excellent with grilled fish and in an accompanying thickened sauce for fried chicken. Lime juice is an important ingredient of many marinades for meat, chicken and veal. It is the correct marinade for making Tahitian raw fish salad. Use in jams, jellies, marmalade and to make many kinds of spicy pickles. Lime juice, sometimes with the grated rind, is used to flavor ice creams, sorbets and cream fillings for cakes and pies.

Food value a fair source of vitamin C.

Longan

This is a large tree of Southeast Asian countries. It bears clusters of small fruits with a brownish skin which surrounds a pulp-covered seed. The pulp has a sweet refreshing flavour.
Store on racks for a few days; longer in refrigerator.
To use peel off skin and eat raw.
Food value quite a good source of vitamin C.

Long Bean (Yard Long Bean)

This tropical climbing legume produces beans 1 ft (30 cm) and more in length. Beans vary in color from dark to pale green and have a distinctive flavor. They are usually marketed in tied bunches.
Store in perforated plastic bags in a cool place, or in the refrigerator, where they will keep in good condition for 3-7 days.
To use trim off the top and stem ends. Arrange beans in a bunch of similar lengths, hold with left hand on a board and with right hand cut beans diagonally into slices with a sharp knife. Alternatively, cut into suitable lengths for cooking. Young thin beans may be cooked whole and then tied or plaited to make an attractive vegetable garnish.
Long beans may be included in any mixed vegetable dish, or cooked, cooled and served as a salad. The flavour of beans is enhanced by a little basil, spring onion or green coriander.
Food value a fair source of vegetable protein, vitamins and minerals. A good family vegetable.

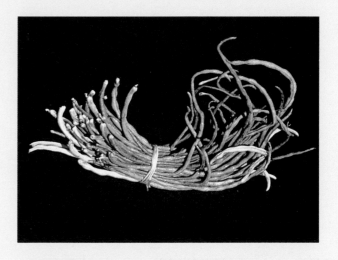

Lychee (Litchi)

The lychee comes from southern China and is now grown in most tropical countries. Bunches of pink, thin-shelled fruits hang from the branches of large trees. Inside the shell a pearl-grey, translucent fruit surrounds a seed. The fruit has a slightly chewy texture and delicious sweet flavour.
Store fresh for a day or two at room temperature in cool weather. Refrigerate for longer storage. The fruits are also dried, pickled and canned.
To use peel off the outer skin and eat fresh. The fruit pulp may also be used in salads, ice creams, sorbets and blended to make cold fruit drinks.
Food value quite a good source of vitamin C.

Mango

Can vary when ripe from those which are small and green to large reddish-yellow or green fruits. Avoid fruits with a stringy texture and turpentine smell. Good-quality fruits have a medium-sized seed and a sweet juicy yellow flesh, similar to a peach. Fruit should be firm and greenish to full yellow-red color, although some good varieties have a green skin even when ripe.
Store in a cool, dark place. Ripe fruit will not last more than two days. Peel ripe mangoes, slice and freeze.
To use cut the base off the fruit and peel downwards. Alternatively, slice off the sides of the fruit and press back skin and the flesh should come out easily. Use raw in fruit salads. Purée raw or cooked ripe fruit and use in ice cream, mousse and gelatin desserts.
Food value a very good source of vitamins C and A. Give mango juice to infants.

Mangosteen

This is a dark reddish purple fruit about the size of a small apple. The dark colored rind surrounds segments of juicy white pulp which adhere to seeds. This is the part eaten. Mangosteen is one of the most delicious of all tropical fruits. The rind contains a red dye which stains.
To use cross-cut the rind from stem to calyx and pull back from the fruit. The dark rind gives the appearance of flower petals which provide a background to the white juicy fruit. Alternatively, cut the rind round the middle of the fruit and scoop pulp out with a spoon. Best eaten raw. The pulp can be removed from seeds and blended to make a juice.
Store ripe fruits on racks in a cool place or refrigerate. Fruit is best eaten as soon as possible.
Food value This fruit's main advantage is its flavour. It has a low food value.

Manioc

(Cassava) Should be cream or light yellow in color. Blue-grey streaks in the flesh indicate that roots are not fresh. Roots should be crisp and break easily. Over-mature roots have a lot of hard fiber.
Store under cool damp conditions. Peeled manioc may be frozen raw.
To use peel, cut in 2½-inch (6-cm) pieces and steam or boil. You must discard cooking water. Use raw grated manioc in bread and biscuit recipes, to make desserts and to thicken gravy or soup. Form into cakes and fry in hot oil. Grate cooked manioc to make a base for fish cakes, cut into sections and fry in hot oil to make crisp chips. Put frozen manioc in boiling water or steam.
Food value manioc has more carbohydrate and less protein in it than other root vegetables. It is however quite a good source of vitamin C. Grated raw manioc makes a good porridge for infants and children when served with milk.

Okra

(Bhindi or Ladies' Fingers) The pods should be round, tender and of even color and about 3 inches (7 cm) long. Over-mature fruit are tough and stringy.

Store in plastic bags in a cool place. Lasts several days. Okra freezes well. Blanch in boiling water for 3 minutes, cool, dry and freeze. Alternatively, stir-fry 5 minutes in a little hot oil and cool, put prepared okra into plastic bags and freeze.

To use trim off short stems without cutting pod. If skin is very 'fuzzy' rib with nylon scraper under cold running water. To avoid sticky texture, sprinkle with vinegar and gently toss to ensure pods are well covered. Leave 30 minutes, wash well and dry. Boil whole in salted water and serve with butter or cold in salads. Cut into 1-inch (2-cm) lengths, mix with tomatoes and fry until tender. One of the main vegetables of curries and widely used in Middle Eastern cooking.

Food value a fair source of vitamins and minerals.

Papaya (Pawpaw)

Fruits should be firm and yellow in color. Select yellow or half-yellow fruits for ripening at home. Green fruit has a poor flavor. When ripened, flesh color and flavor differ according to variety. Size may vary from that of a grapefruit to a small watermelon. Flesh may be pink or orange in color and should be sweet.

Store ripe fruit in a cool place or refrigerator. Half-ripe fruit ripens in a dark cupboard. Freeze fruit purée.

To use cut into sections and scoop out seeds. Score flesh with a knife, sprinkle with lemon or lime juice. Peel ripe fruits, cut into cubes and use in fruit or vegetable salads. Do not add raw fruit to jellies as it contains a substance which breaks down gelatin. Use cooked papaya in pie, soufflé and mousse recipes. Blend ripe flesh to make papaya juice. Papaya is a good tenderizer for tough meat. Use green papaya as a vegetable.

Food value a rich source of vitamins C and A. A good first food for infants.

Passionfruit

Tropical passionfruit has a yellow shiny skin which becomes wrinkled on ripening.

Store in a cool place on wire racks. Fruits will keep a week in cool weather.

To use cut fruits in half and spoon out the pulp. Use the pulp with the seeds or strain. The pulp and seeds are used in fruit salads and cream-type desserts. The strained juice makes a very good fruit drink or addition to other fruit drinks and punches.

Food value a fair source of vitamins C and A.

Pineapple

Some varieties are yellow-orange when ripe while others are brownish green. Fruit must be firm all over with no sign of any damage or bruising as this will affect the texture and flavor.

Store ripe fruit in a cool place. It will last for 2-3 days. In hot weather put fruit into a plastic bag and refrigerate. Always cover cut fruit as it flavors other foods. Freezes well.

To use peel off outer skin. Remove eyes by cutting quarter-inch wedges diagonally along the lines of the eyes. Serve raw as a breakfast fruit or in fruit salads. Countless desserts and ice creams use pineapple as their principal fruit. Do not use raw fruit in gelatin dishes as it contains a substance which destroys gelatin. Pineapple slices or cubes are included in beef, pork or chicken recipes. Raw fruit will help tenderize meat and thus can be used in a marinade or as part of the recipe.

Food value a fair source of vitamin C.

Plantains

(Cooking bananas) The many varieties may be used green, half-ripe or ripe. Color of the flesh varies from cream to dark orange.

Store by hanging a bunch in a cool place or put 'hands' or loose fruit on a wire rack. Undamaged fruit will keep for several days. Ripening takes place during storage.

To use steam, boil or bake green fruits in the skin and peel before serving. Peel green fruit, slice thinly and fry in hot oil to make chips, or roast whole in hot fat around meat. To cook ripe fruits, bake, boil or steam in skin until soft. Remove skin, add coconut cream or grated coconut, simmer for a minute, then serve cold.

Food value similar to bananas. The orange-fleshed fruits are a good source of vitamin A.

Pomelo

This fruit is also known as Pummelo and Pamplemouse. It is a cross between a grapefruit and the tropical Shadock. Fruits can weigh up to a kilogram (2.2lbs) and more. When ripe, color varies between yellow and yellowish-green. The flesh is segmented, a little coarser than that of grapefruit, and varies in color from pale green to yellow or pale pink. Pomelos have a unique refreshing flavor.

Store on racks in a cool place. Fruits will last for two weeks in cool weather. Flavour and juiciness improve with storage. Freeze juice and make whole fruits into jams and marmalades.

To use peel off the skin and pith and eat segments raw. Cut in half and prepare as for grapefruit. Pomelo makes an excellent breakfast fruit. Remove segments and add to fruit salads or to shredded Chinese cabbage to make a salad. Squeeze out juice and make into drinks. Cut up half-ripe fruits and make into marmalade.

Food value a good source of vitamin C.

Rambutan

Has bunches of red or orange fruits, each looking like a large gooseberry covered in fleshy spines. The rind surrounds a melting white pulp and a seed. The fruit has an unusual sweet acid flavour.

Store on wire trays in a cool place or in perforated plastic bags in the refrigerator. Fruit has a short storage life at day temperatures.

To use cut the leathery rind with a sharp knife and pull back from the pulp. This fruit is best eaten fresh. The pulp can be included in fruit salads and ice creams.

Food value a good source of vitamin C.

Sapodilla

This fruit is also known as Sapodilla-plum, Zapote, Bully Tree and Naseberry. The medium-sized tree comes from South America and is now widely grown in tropical countries. It has round or oval, red-brown, thin-skinned fruits. When ripe, the fruit has a mass of luscious brown pulp which surrounds a large black seed.

Store mature fruits till soft and ripe on racks. Ripe fruits are best refrigerated.

To use Fruits should be soft. Peel the skin off ripe fruits and eat fresh. Remove the pulp and use to make ice creams and sorbets. It is important to ensure that the fruit is really ripe. Half-ripe fruits have a sticky consistency.

Food value a fair source of vitamins and minerals.

Soursop

Becomes very soft and the skin turns yellow during ripening. It is best to buy firm fruits and ripen at home. Soursop has a unique flavour which provides desserts and drinks with a distinctive taste.

Store in a cool place till soft. Soursop flesh and purée freezes well. Make into ice cubes.

To use cut in half and peel off soft skin. Rub through a wire strainer to make a thick purée or eat segments fresh. Do not break or eat the large black pips as these contain a toxic substance. Pour the purée over fruit salads. Use in fruit drinks, ice cream, sorbet and gelatin recipes. Combine with egg yolk to make custard. Thicken with a little cornflour, add lime juice and serve as a sauce for ice cream, fruit or cake desserts. Use to flavor whipped cream toppings or fillings. Serve as ice blocks in drinks.

Food value a good source of the vitamins riboflavin and niacin. Makes a good drink for children.

Sweet potato

(Kumara, kumala) Color varies from white to orange or purple. Always choose roots free from holes or rot. White varieties are less sweet than yellow. Purple roots have a very good flavor and texture.

Store in a dry airy place. Keeps for 2-3 weeks.

To use scrub well and steam, bake, or boil in skin. To avoid discoloration after peeling, put into cold water or cook in the skin and then peel. Serve with butter, sour cream and chives. To roast, parboil then peel and cook around meat or in hot fat. Very good with pork. Bake whole, scoop out flesh, season well with lemon juice or port wine, butter, salt and pepper. Refill shells and brown in hot oven. Cooked cubed sweet potato may be used to make salads. Include cooked purée in scones or soufflés. Make sweet potato pie from purée and rich egg custard baked in a pastry shell.

Food value a nutritious carbohydrate food. Good for infants. Yellow varieties provide vitamin A.

Tahitian Apple

This fruit is also known as Ambarella, Otaheite-apple, Wi or Vi apple, Great Hog Plum and Kedondong. It is an oval-shaped fruit and is picked when fully mature and green in color. On ripening the color changes to yellow. Crisp white flesh surrounds a spiny seed. The fruit has a refreshing sweet acid flavor.

Store on racks in a cool place or refrigerate. Fruits can ripen fast at day temperatures. For long storage, freeze cooked fruit or make juice into jelly or jam.

To use peel and cut up fruit to make into raw spicy chutneys or add to fruit salads. Cut up whole green fruits and boil with water till soft, strain off juice and make into jelly or jam. Rub cooked fruit through a sieve to make purée. This may be used in desserts or in a sauce to go with pork.

Food value a good source of vitamin C. The juice and puréed cooked fruit make good foods for small children.

Tangerine

Tangerines belong to the mandarin and orange family. The small round fruits are greenish yellow to bright orange in color and are widely grown in tropical areas of Southeast Asia. Fruits have a loose skin which is easily peeled off. They are very juicy and have a distinct aromatic flavor.

Store on racks in a cool place for a few days. Fruits soften quickly and for longer storage should be refrigerated. Juice and pulp freeze well. Half-ripe tangerines can be made into jam.

To use peel off the skin and separate segments. These are best eaten fresh. Squeeze out the juice to make drinks. Remove pith and seeds from segments and blend to make a purée. Use this in cold gelatin desserts, ice creams and sorbets.

Food value a good source of vitamin C.

Taro

(Dalo) The flesh of the many varieties ranges in color from white to blue-grey. Texture may be fairly dry or moist. Roots should be fresh and firm at the root end.
Store in a cool dry place. Keeps well for several days. Alternatively, place unpeeled whole roots in a plastic bag and seal. Roots will remain fresh for several months. Raw peeled taro may be frozen.
To use bake in the skin or peel and bake whole or in halves, slice and steam or boil. Put frozen pieces directly in boiling water. Cooked taro makes excellent thick or thin chips which remain crisp when cold. Add cubes of prepared taro to fish dishes cooked in coconut cream. Pound cooked taro to make a smooth dough, form into 1-inch (4-cm) balls or cubes. Serve with coconut cream or caramel sauce as a dessert.
Food value a good carbohydrate food providing some minerals, vitamins and protein.

Taro leaves

(Rouru) Pick only young leaves with green stems. Old leaves and those from purple-stemmed varieties contain a substance which irritates the mouth and throat. Some leaves are free from this; in others it can be broken down by rapid boiling in a closed pot.
To store wash and remove stems, put leaves together and roll up. Put in a plastic bag in the refrigerator, or wrapped in a banana leaf in a cool place. Keeps for several days.
To use cook leaves in boiling salted water for 5 minutes, turn over and cook for another 5 minutes. Drain and add butter or coconut cream. Put corned beef and chopped onions on leaves, add coconut cream, wrap up and steam or bake to make palusami. Use puréed leaves in cream soups.
Food value a good source of vitamins C and A and minerals. Provides some protein.

Tropical Squash

Varieties include Chinese marrow, long round, bottle, lauki, luffa, taroi and others. One of the most interesting and varied of vegetables.
Store on racks. Will keep for several days.
To use peel carefully, slice or dice and steam. Serve with white or cheese sauce, or in curries. Round and long squash can be stuffed by carefully cutting off the top, removing seeds and stringy pith and filling with a favourite meat or vegetable stuffing. Oven-bake till tender. Grate or thinly dice crisp varieties and include in salads. Dice and poach in a light syrup flavoured with lemon, cloves, nutmeg or cinnamon and add to fruit salads, or use as a stewed fruit. Sauté in hot butter with cubed pineapple or apple, sweeten with brown sugar, add nutmeg or cinnamon and serve hot or cold as a dessert.
Food value low nutritional value. Should be eaten with legumes, milk, meat or fish.

Watermelon

Fruits are oval or round, and light green or darker variegated green. The flavor and color of the flesh depend on the fruit being mature. A mature fruit should sound hollow when lightly knocked. The inside flesh should be a bright pink color.

Store fruits in any airy cool place. Melons will keep for 4-5 days. Cut fruit should be put in a plastic bag in the refrigerator.

To use cut into slices and eat as fresh fruit. Cut into cubes or make into balls, flavor with lemon juice and mint and serve as a dessert, add to fruit salads, make into sorbet, use in gelatin desserts, cold fish dishes and vegetable salads. Blend to make a refreshing drink. Cut fruit in half, remove the flesh and use the shells as containers for fruit or vegetable salads. Use watermelon balls and cubes as a garnish for drinks, salads and desserts.

Food value watermelon has a low energy value and is a useful fruit for weight watchers.

Winged Beans

Beans should be soft; hard firm ones are not suitable for cutting and slicing. Beans vary from 4-6 inches (10-15 cm) in length.

Store in plastic bags in the refrigerator and use as soon as possible.

To use cut diagonally into slices and cook for 4-5 minutes in boiling salted water or stir-fry. Serve as for long beans. Cold winged beans make an excellent salad. Toss in a coconut cream dressing and flavor with chopped onion and tomato. Use the edible blue flowers as a garnish.

Food value a very good source of vitamins, minerals and protein. Because of their high food value, winged beans are known as a 'wonder food' of the tropics.

Yams

There are many varieties of yams ranging in size from 2-4 pounds (1-2 kg) to 50 pounds (25 kg) or more, and they may be white or purple in color. White yam is fairly similar to the potato in color and texture. Small sweet yams are 6-8 inches (15-20 cm) long. Most yams have a fine texture and flavor.

Store in a cool airy place. Roots will keep for many months under good conditions.

To use peel and slice and then steam or boil. To prevent browning, store peeled yams in water before cooking. Scrub whole yams and puncture before baking in the oven. Serve peeled and slice or scoop out flesh, grate or mash and season with butter, salt and pepper, return to shell and brown in oven. Add minced cooked meat and chopped parsley, cheese or flaked fish and coconut cream to mashed yam. Return to shell and bake. Roast pieces of peeled yam with meat.

Food value similar to taro. Mashed yam is a good infant food.

Roast pork leg with taro cakes and stir-fried vegetables

MANILA PORK

A traditional Filippino way of cooking pork

2-2½ kg (4-5 lb) loin of pork
boiling water
2 cups sugar
1 cup vinegar
1 cup water
1 teaspoon crushed green ginger
1 teaspoon chopped garlic
1 tablespoon cornflour
1 teaspoon salt
¼ cup water

Finely score the skin of the pork using a sharp knife. Pour over a jug of boiling water. Bake at 260ºC (500ºF) for ½ an hour to allow browning. In the meantime make a sweet and sour sauce by combining sugar, vinegar, water, crushed green ginger and chopped garlic in a saucepan. Add cornflour and salt mixed to a paste with water. Stir, bringing to the boil and simmer until thick. Pour the sauce over the pork and bake at 150ºC (300ºF) for an additional 2½ hours.
Serves 6

GLAZED PICKLED PORK

2-2.5 kg (4-5 lb) leg pickled pork
1 bunch fresh herbs
(or 2 teaspoons dried herbs)
2 teaspoons whole cloves
½ cup lemon juice
½ cup orange or pineapple juice
sugar
pineapple or crystallized cherries

Wrap pickled pork in a cloth and place in a large pot or washing boiler. Cover with plenty of water. Add fresh herbs or dried mixed herbs and 2 teaspoons of whole cloves. Bring to the boil and simmer for 2-2½ hours. Take out, remove cloth and peel off the skin. This should pull away easily if the pork is sufficiently cooked. Score the pork with the point of a knife, cross-wise and diagonally. Decorate with whole cloves and pour over juice. Sprinkle generously with sugar. Bake ¾-1 hour at 180º C (350º F) or until golden, basting occasionally. Remove and decorate by inserting pieces of pineapple or crystallized cherry into the skin. Bake a further 10-15 minutes, being careful not to burn the fruit. Serve hot or cold.

Chicken

Chicken is used widely in the tropics and lends itself well to flavourings of herbs and spices. When making stuffings for chicken, use onion, and herbs such as coriander, marjoram, oregano, sage, juniper, thyme and parsley. When roasting, rub the outside and cavity with garlic, rosemary, lemon or soy sauce.

In general, basil, garlic, parsley, ginger, saffron, sesame seed, tarragon, lemon, pineapple add richness to the flavour of chicken, in stews, roasts or casseroles.

MARINADES FOR CHICKEN

Put chicken pieces or cut chicken in a basic lemon marinade for 4-5 hours.

1. ¼ cup lemon juice
½ crushed clove garlic
¼ cup oil
½ teaspoon salt
freshly ground black pepper

a) replace lemon with fresh pineapple juice
b) prepare lemon marinade and add ½ cup of finely chopped ripe pawpaw
c) prepare lemon marinade replacing lemon juice with a dry white or red wine

2. 1 tablespoon soy sauce
¼ cup salad oil
2 teaspoons finely chopped onion
1 teaspoon crushed green ginger

ROAST CHICKEN EASTERN STYLE

Serve with fried pineapple pieces and hot rice salad. For more flavour, replace half cooking oil with sesame oil.

2½ kg (5 lb) chicken
1 crushed clove garlic
2 teaspoons crushed green ginger
1 tablespoon soy sauce
¼ cup oil

Wash and dry chicken. Blend garlic, ginger, soy sauce and oil. Brush cavity and outside of chicken with marinade. Bake at 180ºC (350ºF) basting several times till golden brown.

CHICKEN CURRY

1 kg (2 lb) raw chicken
(cut off the bone)
1 medium onion
3 tablespoons oil
1 teaspoon fennel seeds
3 cloves
5 cardamom pods
1 2cm stick cinnamon
1 stem curry leaves
½ teaspoon chopped green ginger
3 crushed cloves garlic
1 teaspoon turmeric powder
1 teaspoon chilli powder
2 teaspoons curry powder
1 teaspoon salt
2 cups water
2 sprigs parsley or coriander

Cut boned chicken into 4 cm (2 in) cubes. Chop onion and heat oil. When hot, add fennel seeds, cardamom pods and stick of cinnamon. Stir fry until seeds are golden. Add chopped onion, and curry leaves. Stir fry for a couple of minutes more. Add green ginger and crushed garlic cloves. Cook for 3 minutes. Add chicken followed by turmeric powder, chilli powder and curry powder. Add 1 teaspoon salt, or to taste. Cook slowly for 10 minutes. Add sufficient water to half cover. Cover with lid and cook until tender. Add 2 sprigs of coriander for flavour. Remove from heat and serve. If desired remove whole spice before serving. Serve with rice and roti.
Serves 6

Variation
Use 1.75 kg (3 lb) chicken cut into pieces. (In Asia chicken is often cut into pieces with a cleaver. This means that bones will be included.)

Chicken with eggplant stuffing

GOLDEN CHICKEN

2½ kg (5 lb) whole or chicken pieces
1 teaspoon ground pepper
1½ teaspoons ground ginger
3 cardamom pods
1 teaspoon salt
2 teaspoons ground turmeric
3 small onions finely chopped

1 cup yoghurt
½ cup cream

Prick the skin of the chicken with a fork and then rub with a mixture of pepper and ground ginger. Truss bird or put pieces on baking tray and place in an oven at 180° C

(350° F) for 10 minutes. Pound cardamom pods in a bowl, add salt, ground turmeric, chopped onion, yoghurt and cream. Pour over chicken and bake at low heat for 1½ hours or until tender. Baste frequently with sauce.
Serves 6

TROPICAL CHICKEN CASSEROLE

Using taro leaves, beet leaves or spinach.

1 kg (2 lb) chicken
1 lemon
¼ cup oil
salt
pepper
½ cup seasoned flour
¼ cup oil (additional)
2 cups thick coconut cream
1 teaspoon salt
¼ teaspoon pepper
**1 chilli finely chopped
(optional)**
750 gms (1½ lb) taro or beet leaves
2 medium onions
2-3 medium tomatoes

Cut raw boned chicken into 2 cm (1 in) cubes. Marinate for several hours in lemon juice, and oil. Season with salt and pepper. Drain then roll in seasoned flour. Heat additional oil and fry until golden brown. Season thick coconut cream, with salt and pepper and finely chopped chilli. Wash leaves, remove the stems and coarse veins. Finely chop onions.
Place a layer of leaves in casserole, cover with chicken pieces and sprinkle with onion. Pour a little of the coconut cream over the chicken. Repeat the layers making sure that the leaves are used for the last layer. Slice the tomatoes and place on top of the leaves. Cover the casserole and bake 40-50 minutes at 180º C (350º F). Serve with wedges of lemon.
Serves 6

STUFFED CHICKEN LEGS

An unusual and easily prepared dish which is ideal for a party.

12 chicken legs
¼ cup oil
3 tablespoons lemon juice
clove garlic
freshly ground black pepper
salt

1 cup cooked spinach or taro leaves
¼ teaspoon nutmeg
2 teaspoons butter or coconut cream

Insert the tip of a sharp knife in the top of the legs. Separate the flesh from the bone by making a "pocket".
Marinate the legs using a well mixed combination of the oil, lemon juice, crushed garlic, salt and black pepper. Leave for about 4 hours.
Mash cooked spinach till smooth and stir in nutmeg and butter or coconut cream. Season with salt. Put about 1 tablespoon of spinach mixture inside the pocket of each leg. Place legs in baking dish, brush with oil, bake at 190º C (375º F) for 15-20 minutes or until brown. Serve with fresh tomato sauce, rice and salad
Serves 6-8

CHICKEN LOLO SUVU

This delicious, spicy recipe from Burma, using dhal (split peas), and coconut cream. It needs to be made over 2 days. Excellent for a buffet meal.

Preparation of Dhal

250 gms (8 oz) split peas
2 cups water

Soak split peas in water overnight. Strain, wash, add fresh water and bring to boil. Simmer until soft and mushy. Sieve. Refrigerate until required.

Preparation of Chicken

2½ kg (5 lb) chicken
2½ cups water
10 cloves garlic
salt
1 tablespoon crushed green ginger
1½ cups finely chopped onion
5 tablespoons butter
2½ tablespoons curry powder
2 teaspoons ground turmeric
**250 gm (8 oz) peeled fresh tomatoes
(or canned tomatoes)**
1 cup prepared stock
2 chicken stock cubes

Section chicken removing flesh from back and breast. Leave flesh on legs, wings, etc. Prepare stock using back, breast, neck and water. Strain stock and then reduce to one cup by boiling. Reserve. Mash garlic with enough salt to take up moisture. This should yield one round tablespoon of garlic plus salt. Melt butter in a large frypan. Add onions and fry till golden. Stir in curry powder, ground turmeric and prepared garlic and ginger. Cook for 1 minute. Stir in chicken pieces and fry until brown. Add mashed tomatoes, reserved chicken stock and chicken cubes. Simmer until just tender. Remove from heat and refrigerate until next day to allow flavour to fully develop. Do not combine dhal with chicken until ready to use.

Day of Dinner

1 cup thick coconut cream
4 large onions
oil
500 gm white rice

Prepare thick coconut cream. Thinly slice large onions and fry in a minimum amount of oil until slightly golden and transparent. Drain well on paper, place on fresh paper and put in a very low oven to dry until crisp. Keep warm until ready to serve. Cook rice

Assemble Chicken Lolo Suvu by heating chicken thoroughly ½ hour before serving. Stir in dhal and continue stirring until a smooth mixture is achieved. 5 minutes before serving add coconut cream. Do not allow the mixture to boil after coconut cream has been added as fat will separate. If a more soup-like mixture is desired, more chicken broth or thick coconut cream may be added.
Serves 10

**Right above: South seas
pineapple chicken**

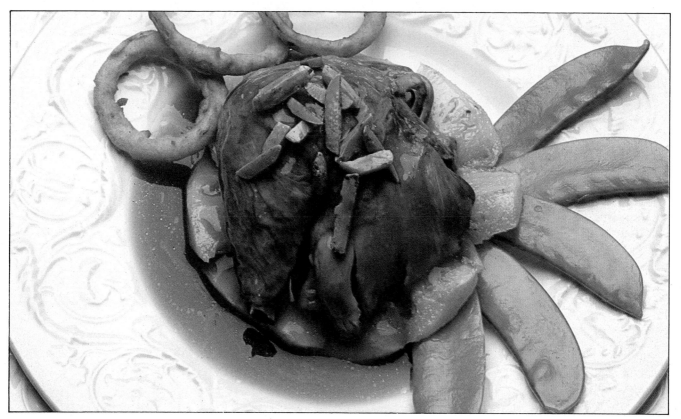

SOUTH SEAS PINEAPPLE CHICKEN

2 kg (4 lb) chicken pieces
¼ cup soy sauce
¼ cup white wine
(medium dry)
juice of 1 lemon or lime
2 teaspoons sesame oil
1 clove garlic
1 teaspoon curry powder
1 teaspoon finely chopped ginger
¼ teaspoon thyme
¼ teaspoon oregano
¼ teaspoon rosemary
freshly ground black pepper
4 medium onions finely sliced
4 tablespoons butter
8 slices pineapple
½ cup toasted almonds
¼ cup white wine
cooked rice

Place chicken in a flat dish and prepare a marinade from soy sauce, wine, lime or lemon juice, sesame oil, crushed garlic, curry powder, ginger, thyme, oregano, rosemary, pepper and pour over the meat. Marinate for several hours, turning at least twice.

Heat butter in a pan and fry onion slices until golden. Remove. Drain the meat (keep marinade) and dust with flour. Heat 2 tablespoons butter in a pan and brown meat on both sides. Pour over the marinade, arrange onion slices on top, cover and simmer for 45 minutes, uncovering for last 15 minutes. Saute the pineapple slices in butter till golden brown.

Serve the chicken on a platter garnished with pineapple slices and almonds. Add ¼ cup wine to pan juices and simmer briefly. Pour over meat or serve separately. Serve with rice.

Variation

Thicken sauce with a little cornflour. Take out onion rings, dip in milk and flour and fry till crisp. Serve with chicken. (Chicken may be substituted with pork chops.)
Serves 6

EGGPLANT STUFFING FOR ROAST CHICKEN

(Makes enough for one large chicken)

2-3 tablespoons oil
1 rasher bacon, chopped
1 small onion, chopped
½ clove garlic
1½ cups eggplant, peeled and diced
½ cup cooked rice
2 tablespoons tomato puree
¼ teaspoon dried coriander
½ teaspoon grated lemon rind
salt and pepper to taste

Heat oil in frypan, add bacon and onion and saute till golden. Add garlic and eggplant. Stir fry until eggplant is cooked, but not too soft. Add rice, tomato puree, coriander and lemon rind. Stir well. Season to taste with salt and pepper.

Variation

Add ¼ cup sultanas or currants with eggplant.

Vegetables

Many tropical vegetables have a good flavour and texture but as with all vegetables, proper preparation and cooking must be used to get the best results.

All the dark green leafy spinach-type vegetables like taro leaves (rourou), can be used raw in salads or quickly cooked in a little water or butter. These vegetables and the red and yellow fruits like pumpkin and sweet peppers, have a high vitamin content.

Most tropical beans and gourd-type vegetables like cucumber, and Chinese marrow have the same food values as their temperate climate equivalents.

Starchy root vegetables like cassava, and taro make a pleasant change from potatoes and in most recipes can be substituted. Excellent for potato and other salads. Cassava makes particularly good chips which retain their crispness.

The flavour of many vegetables can be enhanced with a sauce or dressing. Some suggestions may be found in Dressings and Accompaniments.

Taro cakes

CASSAVA or TARO CAKES

3 cups mashed or grated cooked cassava/taro
2 teaspoons grated onion
2 teaspoons chopped parsley
1 egg
salt and pepper
flour
oil

Mash or grate sufficient cooked cassava or taro. Put in a bowl and add onion, parsley, beaten egg, salt and pepper. Mix well. Form into cakes, roll in flour. Fry in hot oil on both sides till golden brown. Serve with meat and vegetables.

Variation
Replace 1 cup of cassava or taro with 1 cup of flaked cooked fish or mince meat. Serve meat or fish cakes with fresh tomato sauce.

54

COCONUT SPICED VEGETABLES

The coconut and spices in this recipe enhance the flavour of the fresh vegetables. An excellent vegetarian dish.

6 cups of vegetables cut in strips (use fairly firm vegetables such as celery, carrots, beans, Chinese cabbage or beet stalks, snow peas (sugarsnap), Chinese marrow or cucumber.
½ cup grated coconut
1 cup water
1 teaspoon cumin seed

1 clove garlic
1 chilli
½ cup thick coconut cream
salt to taste
4-6 curry leaves

Put about 2 cups of water in a saucepan with salt and bring to the boil. Cook each kind of vegetable separately till just tender, remove from the saucepan using the same water to cook the other vegetables. Extra water may have to be added as the cooking proceeds. (About three or four different kinds of vegetables are suffi-

cient to give a good flavour to this dish).

Put one cup of vegetable water, the coconut, cumin, garlic and chilli in a blender and reduce to a fine sauce. Put this into the saucepan with the vegetable water, coconut cream, and curry leaves and simmer for 5 minutes. Add vegetables, salt to taste and simmer another 5 minutes.

Note: 3 tablespoons of desiccated coconut may be used in place of

Coconut spiced vegetables

the fresh. If no blender is available, pound the coconut and spices together with a little of the water and then add the remainder.
Serves 6

SWEET POTATO SOUFFLE

3 cups mashed sweet potato
2 tablespoons butter · melted
1 tablespoon milk
2 tablespoons grated onion
½ teaspoon cinnamon
salt and pepper
1 tablespoon melted butter
3 eggs

Mash cooked potato till very smooth. There should be no lumps. Add melted butter, milk, onion, cinnamon, salt and pepper to taste. Mix well. Separate the eggs and beat the whites till stiff, then beat the yolks till frothy. Fold first the egg yolks into the potato mixture, and then the egg whites. Put into a round baking dish, preferably a souffle dish, brush the top with melted butter and bake in a pan of water at 160ºC (325ºF) for about 30 to 40 minutes, or till the souffle is well risen and golden brown. Very good with pork or cold meats.
Serves 6

TOMATO CUPS

An attractive vegetable dish using spinach or taro leaves. May be served alone or with meat.

6 large tomatoes
1½ cups cooked spinach or taro leaves (rourou)
2 tablespoons thick coconut cream
¼ teaspoon nutmeg
salt to taste

Cut the tops of the tomatoes evenly or make a serated edge with the point of a sharp knife. Scoop out the pulp. Mash spinach or taro leaves (rourou) with a fork, add coconut cream, nutmeg and salt to taste. Put mixture into the tomato

cups and place in a shallow baking dish. Cover with foil and bake in moderate oven for about 10 minutes. Do not overcook as tomatoes will lose their shape.
Serves 3-6 depending on accompaniments

SAVOURY BREADFRUIT

This tasty recipe has its origins in the West Indies.

1 large breadfruit
2 tablespoons oil
2 chopped spring onions
1 medium onion, chopped
2 capsicums chopped
(use red and green for colour)
2 tablespoons chopped parsley
1 tablespoon herbs, chopped
(or 1 teaspoon dried mixed herbs)
1 cup cooked meat, cubed
(pork, ham or corned beef)
1 cup of beef stock
1 cup cooked cubed carrots
salt and pepper
1 egg

Wash the breadfruit and puncture several times. Bake in moderate oven for about 1½ hours, or till soft. Heat oil and saute spring onions, chopped onion and capsicum for 5 minutes. Add chopped herbs and cook another few minutes. Add meat which should be cut in 1 cm (½ inch) cubes and stock and simmer for 15 minutes. Cut the top off the breadfruit and scoop out the inside pulp leaving about 1 cm (½ inch) attached to the skin. Grate the pulp, put all the ingredients in a bowl, add 1 beaten egg and mix well. Put the mixture back inside the shell. Attach the top with a skewer or toothpick and wrap the breadfruit in foil or a softened banana leaf. Bake in a hot oven for 30-40 minutes. Serve cut in slices with a mushroom or brown sauce flavoured with capsicums.
Serves 6-8

OKRA GUMBO

Gumbo is very good served alone, with other dishes or with lamb or corned beef.

1 rasher bacon
2 cups chopped onion
1½ cups chopped capsicum
18 young okra pods
5 tomatoes
1 cup corn, fresh or canned
salt and pepper

Cut up bacon and fry till crisp, add onion and capsicum and fry for 5 minutes, stirring all the time. Clean okra pods. Peel and quarter tomatoes and add both to the mixture in the pan. Simmer 10 minutes or till dry. Stir in well drained cooked corn. Season to taste and continue simmering for 10 minutes. It is important to retain just enough moisture to stop the mixture sticking.
Serves 5-6

FRESH CASSAVA
OR TARO CAKES

2 cups freshly grated cassava/taro
1 tablespoon grated onion
salt and pepper to taste
flour
oil

Mix onion, salt and pepper with cassava or taro. Form into cakes about 1 cm (½ in) thick on a floured board. Fry in hot oil till golden brown on both sides. Drain well on paper and serve with meat and vegetables.

STUFFED EGGPLANT
(Aubergine)

3 medium eggplants
1 medium onion
1 clove garlic
½ teaspoon ground coriander
¼ cup oil
250 gms (½ lb) minced mutton or beef

Stuffed eggplant

1 tablespoon chopped parsley
½ cup soft breadcrumbs
or cooked rice
2 tablespoons tomato puree
salt and pepper
1 egg

Cut the eggplants in half and scoop out the inside flesh leaving about ½ cm (¼ in) on the inside. Arrange in a casserole. Chop the onion, crush the garlic. Put oil in a pan and heat. Saute the onion, garlic and coriander. Add the mince and chopped flesh of egg-plant. Saute for about 5 minutes and add parsley, salt and pepper, and finally breadcrumbs or rice and tomato puree. Stir well. Cook for several more minutes and then remove from heat. Beat the egg and mix into the ingredients. Fill the eggplant shells with the mixture. Cover with foil, or a lid, and bake in moderate oven for 45 minutes. Take off the cover, brush with a little oil and brown.
Serve hot with fresh tomato sauce or cold with salad and tomato dressing (see page 23).

Variation
Mix ½ cup tomato puree with 1 cup of water or stock. Season with salt and pepper and pour round the stuffed eggplants before baking.
Note: Any leftover meat, beans, tomato mixtures may be used in this recipe.
Serves 6

TARO WITH COCONUT CREAM

2 cups taro peeled diced and boiled
1 cup prawns peeled
2 cups coconut cream
1 onion peeled and finely sliced
30 gm (1 oz) butter
2 cloves garlic crushed
salt and pepper to taste

Melt butter and saute the garlic, onions and prawns, for 3 minutes. Add coconut cream and stir until nearly boiling. do not allow coconut cream to boil. Add taro and seasoning. Reheat before serving.

TARO FISH CAKES

300 gm (10 oz) can salmon or tuna
450 gm (14 oz) taro
2 eggs
salt and pepper to taste
flour for dusting
breadcrumbs

Peel, boil, and mash the taro. Beat in 2 egg yolks and seasoning. Mix in salmon and form into flat cakes. Dust with seasoned flour, brush with 2 egg whites and coat with crisp breadcrumbs. Fry in a little hot butter or bake for about 15 minutes on a well greased and heated baking tray, in a moderately hot oven, or 25 minutes in a moderate oven. Serve with cheese sauce (see Vegetable Cheese Pie).

TARO DUCHESS

500 gm (1 lb) taro
1 egg
30 gm (1 oz) butter
salt and pepper

Peel, slice, boil and mash taro. Beat in the egg yolk, butter and seasoning. using a piping bag with a 2 cm (¾ in) rose, pipe in large rosettes on a baking tray. Brush with a little beaten egg and bake at 220ºC (400ºF) until golden.

BAKED TARO with CHEESE

1 clove garlic
1 kg (2 lb) taro
1 teaspoon salt
freshly ground black pepper
200 gm (6 oz) Swiss cheese grated
70 gm (2 oz) butter
1 cup (250 ml) milk
caraway seeds (optional)

Rub a baking dish with the garlic before buttering it. Peel the taros and slice them finely. Place in a bowl of cold water to remove some of the starch. Drain and dry on kitchen paper. Spread half the taro slices on the bottom of the dish. Season with salt and pepper and half the grated cheese. Dot with half the butter. Sprinkle with caraway seeds. Arrange the other half of the taro slices over the first and season. Sprinkle other half of grated cheese over taros. Bring milk to the boil and pour over the taro. Place in a pre-heated 200ºC (400ºF) oven and bake until taros are tender, milk has been absorbed and the top is golden.

TARO with PORK & TOMATO

This recipe originated in Cyprus. Taro is a well known food in Egypt and was taken from there to Cyprus.

½ kg (1 lb) taro
1 kg (2 lb) pork
¼ cup oil
1 large onion
1 clove garlic crushed
1 cup chopped green capsicum
½ cup chopped celery
1½ cups tomato puree
½ teaspoon salt
½ teaspoon sugar
2 tablespoon lemon juice
freshly ground black pepper
garnish of chopped parsley or green coriander

Peel taro and cut into quarters, then cut into slices ½ cm (¼ in) thick. Cut pork into cubes about 2

cm (1 in) cubes. Heat the oil and saute the pork till brown. Remove from pan. New saute the onion till clear and add chopped green capsicum, celery and garlic, stirring well for a few minutes. Add the pork and tomato puree to the vegetables and simmer for 20-30 minutes. Arrange the taro slices on top of the prk, sprinkle with lemon juice and then black pepper. Cover and simmer for about 30 minutes over low heat, till pork and taro are soft. Garnish with chopped parsley or corainder.
Serves 6-8

COCONUT SCALLOPED TARO

1 kg prepared taro
½ cup thick coconut cream
½ cup water
½ small onion grated
½ teaspoon salt
1 tablespoon lemon juice
½ cup grated coconut

Cut taro into slices ½ cm (¼ in) thick and arrange in a flat casserole dish. Mix coconut cream, water, grated onion, salt and lemon juice and pour over the taro. Cover with foil and bake for about 45 minutes in a medium oven or till taro is soft. Remove the foil, sprinkle with grated coconut and brown under the grill. Serve with meat or other vegetables.

Variation
Omit grated coconut and garnish with chopped spring onion or parsley.

TARO & CHICKEN COCONUT CREAM CASSEROLE

1 kg (2 lb) chicken pieces
1 large onion chopped
250 grams (½ lb) spinach
or taro leaves
1 kg (2 lb) taro

185 grams (6 oz) tomatoes
2 teaspoons cornflour
1 425 ml (14 fl oz) can coconut cream
and ½ can water
(or 2 grated coconuts made into 600
ml (1 pint) cream)
1 teaspoon salt
lemon slices

Arrange alternate layers of chicken, chopped onion, spinach or taro leaves cut into ½ cm (¼ in) thick slices in a casserole. Mix coconut cream with salt and cornflour and pour over the top. Cover the top of the casserole with sliced tomatoes. Cover with foil or a lid and bake at 160ºC (325ºF) for 1 hour. Serve with lemon slices. Serves 6 - 8.

TARO, PINEAPPLE & BACON

An attractive dish for a buffet meal

500 gm (1 lb) taro
4 slices pineapple
4 slices bacon
4 spring onions
1 tablespoon butter
1 tablespoon oil
4 spring onions
freshly ground black pepper

Steam or boil taro slices till just cooked. Drain and put aside till cool, then cut into chips 2 cm (1 in) long and 1 cm (½ in) wide. Cut pineapple into wedges and bacon slices into several pieces. Chop the spring onions.

Put oil and butter into a heavy pan and heat. Fry the taro till golden, and drain on paper, saute the pineapple pieces till golden and, lastly, fry the bacon till crisp. Combine taro, bacon and pineapple, toss with chopped spring onion and black pepper and serve immediately.
Serves 6.

Taro pineapple and bacon

59

Pancakes

The versatility of pancakes earns them special attention. Simple to make, they can be filled with either a sweet or savoury filling and used for entrees, main courses or desserts. Spicy or fruity tropical fillings make pancakes a quick and interesting meal or addition to a menu.

Pancakes may be prepared ahead of time, cooled and stacked with greaseproof paper between layers. Or they may be placed in a plastic bag and refrigerated for up to 48 hours or even frozen for 3 to 4 weeks. A great time saver when entertaining.

BASIC PANCAKES (CREPES)

This recipe is suitable for both savoury and sweet pancakes. For savoury pancakes leave out the sugar.

1 cup flour
1 tablespoon sugar
pinch of salt
3 eggs
2 tablespoons butter melted
1½ cups milk

Stir flour, sugar (omit sugar if making savoury pancakes) and salt together. Beat eggs into flour mixture, one at a time, beating well after each addition. Melt butter, blend with milk, slowly beat into flour mixture. Leave to stand for 2 hours. Lightly butter a very hot 25 cm (10 inch) heavy frypan (cast-iron is best) for large pancakes or 12 cm (5 inch) pan for smaller ones. Pour ¼ cup of batter into a large pan, or about 2 tablespoons into a small one, tilt pan around until batter is evenly distributed and ceases to run. When it is dry on top with fine bubbles, flip it over with the help of a spatula or fish slice. Cook for a minute more. Remove to wire rack to keep warm. Stack succeeding pancakes. Cover with greaseproof and clean towel and heat in oven at 150ºC (300ºF) for 10 minutes.

Makes 12 large or 24 small crepes.

SPINACH CHEESE PANCAKES

Spinach may be substituted with taro leaves

12 basic pancakes
1 cup cooked finely chopped spinach or taro leaves
2 rashers bacon
1 medium onion
2 tablespoons butter
2 tablespoons flour
½ teaspoon salt
dash pepper
½ teaspoon dried mustard
1 cup milk
½ cup finely grated cheese (cheddar or gruyere)

Prepare cooked finely chopped green leaves. Chop bacon and onion and place in a saucepan and stir fry until bacon is crisp. Remove bacon and onion, and toss with leaves.

Prepare sauce by melting butter and stirring flour, salt, pepper, and dry mustard. Slowly stir in milk cooking over slow heat until the sauce is thick and smooth. Stir in cheese and reduce heat. Divide leaf mixture between pancakes, allowing about 2 tablespoons each. Place the mixture in the middle of the pancake, roll up and place on plates. Allow two pancakes per person. Pour cheese sauce over and serve.

Serves 6

SEAFOOD CREPES

Basic pancake recipe omitting sugar
½ seafood sauce recipe (see page 14)
lemon juice
parsley

Prepare pancakes. Fill and roll with seafood mixture. Sprinkle with lemon juice and finely chopped parsley.
Serves 4

SPINACH SOUR CREAM PANCAKES

12 large pancakes
1 cup cooked finely chopped spinach or taro leaves
2 rashers bacon
half medium onion
2 tablespoons butter
salt and pepper to taste
300 ml (½ pint) sour cream

Prepare cooked and chopped leaves. Finely chop bacon and onion. Melt butter in a saucepan, add onion and bacon and stir fry until bacon is crisp. Stir in sour cream and leaves and add seasoning. Place about 1½ tablespoons of mixture on each pancake, roll up, reheat and serve. Serves 6

COCONUT CREAM CHOCOLATE CREPES

A very easy but impressive dessert

12 basic pancakes
1 cup freshly whipped cream
1 cup freshly grated coconut
100 grams (3 oz) dark chocolate nuts

Prepare pancakes and keep hot. Mix whipped cream and freshly grated coconut, spread liberally on pan-cakes and roll up. Melt dark chocolate over low heat and pour a little over each pancake and decorate with chopped nuts. Serve immediately.
Serves 6

LEMON BANANA CREPES

12 basic pancakes
½ cup mashed banana
½ cup thick cream

Coconut cream chocolate crepes

1 tablespoon lemon juice
1 tablespoon castor sugar

Prepare pancakes and keep hot. Mix mashed banana, cream, lemon juice and castor sugar together. Spread liberally on pancakes. Roll up and sprinkle with a little castor sugar.
Serves 6

Desserts

A well chosen dessert makes the perfect ending to a meal. The choice is important because the flavour and texture should provide contrast to earlier dishes. It is a good idea to serve a simple fruit salad if rich recipes are used in earlier courses. A wide variety of desserts is contained in this section to allow you to choose one to complement your main course. They have been chosen because of their fine flavour and ease of preparation. Many of the recipes may be prepared ahead of time and stored in the refrigerator.

Tropical fruit salads make a very refreshing final course for a lunch or dinner menu, and are particularly good for children and the diet conscious.

TROPICAL FRUIT IN INTERESTING WAYS

Vary the flavour of fruits by serving with a sauce or syrup made from another fruit of complementary flavour. The following suggestions will enable you to make a series of delicious desserts by simply combining two or three fruits. To make a more elaborate dessert, fold in some whipped cream and set with a little gelatin, using 1 tablespoon of gelatin to 3 cups of mixture. (Remember raw pawpaw and pineapple prevent gelatin from setting).

PUREES AND SAUCES

Soursop
Mash the pulp of a ripe fruit and then rub through a sieve. Mix with banana slices.

Orange
Blend orange segments and then sieve. Combine with pawpaw cubes and slices of poached guava.

Guava Puree
Scoop out the seeds and pulp from ripe fruits, add a little water and cook till soft. Rub through a sieve and flavour with lemon and a little sugar. Serve with banana slices.

Avocado, Honey, Lime Sauce
Blend or sieve ripe avocado until creamy. Flavour with lime or lemon juice and honey or sugar. Mix with a little whipped cream and serve as a sauce with other fruit, or with ice cream.

SYRUPS

Make a basic syrup by boiling 1 cup of sugar with 1½ cups water and the thin outer skin of ¼ lemon and ¼ orange. Strain through a cloth and store in the refrigerator.

Lemon and Mint
Boil syrup with ½ cup chopped fresh mint, add lemon juice and strain. Serve with melon balls or pineapple cubes.

Orange, Ginger.
Add orange juice and a little finely chopped crystallized ginger to a basic syrup and serve with pawpaw, banana or pineapple.

FRUIT SALADS

To improve the flavour of a mixed fruit salad add 1 cubed ripe tomato and 1 tablespoon whisky or brandy.

Melon Ball Salad
Serve watermelon balls inside half a small rock melon. Flavour with lemon mint syrup.

Ginger Fruit Salad
Add chopped crystallized ginger to rock melon, pineapple or pawpaw fruit salads.

TOASTED COCONUT FRUIT SALAD

Arrange sliced fruits around vanilla ice cream. Top the ice cream with toasted coconut.

FLAVOURED CREAM

Serve fruit salads with flavoured whipped cream. Add 2 teaspoons of a liqueur such as Creme de Menthe, Grenadine, Curacao, Cointreau or rum to a cup of whipped cream. Sweeten cream with icing sugar and flavour with vanilla essence or lemon essence and a little grated lemon rind. Chopped nuts, crystallized ginger or glace cherries may be added to cream.

Melon balls

MINTED PINEAPPLE

1 medium pineapple
1 fresh lime
½ small cup Creme de Menthe
sweetened cream
green colouring
fresh mint leaves

Cut ripe pineapple into bite sized pieces. Sprinkle with the juice of fresh lime and Creme de Menthe. Add extra Creme de Menthe for a stronger mint flavour. Cover and leave in the refrigerator for at least 1 hour. Serve in glasses topped with cream which has been tinted with a little green colouring and fresh mint leaves.
Serves 6

COCONUT GLAZED FRUIT

A delicious cold dessert topped with toasted coconut

Sauce
½ cup sugar
3 tablespoons cornflour
¼ teaspoon salt
1¼ cups water
1 egg
2 tablespoons lemon juice
½ teaspoon grated lemon rind
2 tablespoons butter

Combine sugar, cornflour, salt and water. Stir and cook over medium heat for 5 minutes, or until thick and smooth. Beat egg. Slowly beat in a little of the cornflour mixture, then add to remaining mixture in pan. Cook over low heat for one minute. Remove from stove and cool slightly. Add lemon juice, grated lemon rind and butter.

Fruit
1½ cups cubed pineapple
1½ cups just ripe pawpaw
1 cup sliced banana

Place prepared fruit in a bowl and pour sauce over the top.
Refrigerate until thoroughly chilled and ready to serve.

Toasted Coconut
Grate coconut finely, or use desiccated coconut. Place a thin layer on a tray in a medium oven. Turn frequently till crisp and golden brown. Cover fruit with coconut just before serving.
Serves 8

Mixed fruit salad with melon balls, Minted pineapple, Banana soursop

GRILLED FRUIT

Use fresh fruit

pineapple
apple
pawpaw
mango
banana
2 tablespoons brandy
2 tablespoons honey
1 tablespoons lemon juice
300 ml (½ pint) fresh cream
2 passionfruit
cream

Prepare sufficient fruit to fill 8 skewers. Thread fruit attractively on skewers, with variation in colour. Mix together brandy, honey and lemon juice. Brush fruit. Place fruit underneath the grill and grill for 10 minutes, turning frequently and brushing with marinade. Whip cream, carefully fold in passionfruit. Serve with grilled fruit, allowing 2 fruit skewers per person.
Serves 4

FLAMING FRUIT

Fruits such as ripe mangoes, pineapple and bananas, may be served in this way. Raw fruit should be first dipped in sugar and then placed in a warm dish, or chafing dish, and left in a warm oven for a few minutes. Heat brandy in a spoon or ladle over a candle. Remember, the brandy will not light unless it is warm.

POACHED FRUIT

An attractive way to serve a variety of fruits. Particularly suitable for the firmer fleshed varieties like guava and pineapple.

1 cup sugar
2 cups water
2 tablespoons lemon juice
lemon rind
3 cups prepared fruit

Put sugar, water, lemon juice and rind in a saucepan and bring to the

Grilled fruit

boil. Simmer for a few minutes. Add the prepared fruit which should be cut into attractive strips or slices or cubes. Keep at simmering point till the fruit is just soft but not mushy. Soft fruits like pawpaw and mango should be just put into boiling syrup for a minute or two. Remove from heat, drain off the syrup. When cool, return fruit to syrup.

Variations
Guava with lemon
Pineapple with pawpaw and lemon
Mango with orange
Mango, pawpaw and pineapple
Pawpaw with passionfruit syrup
A mixture of fruits including dried prunes and apricots

FRUIT LOTE

3 cups water
¾ cup grated cassava
(or ½ cup sago)
½ cup sugar
1 cup sliced banana
1 cup diced raw pawpaw
1 cup diced pineapple
¼ cup lemon juice

Mix water, sugar and grated cassava, or sago. Stir mixture well and bring to boil. Add the prepared fruit and cook for 2-3 minutes. Remove from heat and allow to cool. Stir in lemon juice.
Note: If mixture thins, mix ½ cup of mixture with ¼ cup grated cassava and add to remainder in saucepan. Stir well over heat till thick. Serve chilled with thick coconut cream.
Serves 8

TROPICAL FRUIT MOUSSE

Many tropical fruits may be used to make delicious frozen desserts. Fruit mousses are easy to make and can be varied according to the fruit in season. An excellent dinner party dessert.

1 cup fruit pulp
(ripe mango, pawpaw is ideal)
½ cup castor sugar
2 cups whipped cream
2 teaspoons gelatine
2 tablespoons water
1 tablespoon lemon juice

Combine fruit pulp, lemon juice and sugar. Mix water and gelatine in a small metal bowl and melt over boiling water. Add to fruit mixture. Fold into whipped cream adding extra fruit pulp if needed for flavour. Pour into a mould, cover with a plastic wrap or waxed paper and freeze until firm.

Fruit lote

Variations
1. 1 cup sieved cooked mango or pawpaw and 1 tablespoon lemon juice
2. 1 cup crushed pineapple and 1 tablespoon lemon juice
3. ½ cup soursop puree and ½ cup mashed ripe avocado
4. ½ cup orange segments and ½ cup mashed ripe banana
5. 1 cup mashed ripe banana and 1 tablespoon lemon juice
6. 1 cup soursop puree and ½ tablespoon lemon juice

Pineapple glace

and chill thoroughly. Just before serving add one large scoop of ice-cream to each serving and sprinkle liberally with grated chocolate.
Serves 4

PINEAPPLE GLACE

3-4 small pineapples
sugar
Cointreau
(or any orange liqueur)
ice-cream, vanilla

Choose 3-4 evenly shaped small pineapples. (Half a fruit should be sufficient for one serving.) Keep the tops on the fruits, wash well and then cut in half lengthwise. Scoop out the fruit leaving 1 cm (½ inch) flesh around the shell. Sprinkle with sugar and Cointreau and chill for two hours. Finely cut the flesh from inside the pineapple and combine with ice cream. Fill the shells with the mixture and place in plastic bags or a covered container and freeze for at least two hours.
Serves 6-8

TROPICAL GELATO

Delicious with sliced banana or just by itself.

1 cup milk
½ cup sugar
1 teaspoon gelatine
1 tablespoon cold water
2 tablespoons lemon juice
1 cup guava juice, passionfruit or mango pulp, or a blend of the two fruits

Heat milk with sugar, stirring until sugar is dissolved. Dissolve gelatine in cold water and add to hot milk. Mix lemon juice with fruit, fruit juice or pulp, then slowly beat into milk mixture. Place in freezer tray and freeze until mushy. Beat well and refreeze until firm.
Serves 4-6

AVOCADO CHOCOLATE CREAM

1 large avocado
¼ cup sugar
¼ cup lemon juice

4 scoops vanilla ice-cream
grated chocolate

Peel, mash and sieve or blend the avocado. Add sugar and lemon juice. Place in four serving dishes,

TROPICAL FRUIT BASKETS

This simple and attractive dessert with a brandy-snap base can be made from a variety of fruits. Choose fresh fruits of complementary colours.

Baskets

60 gm (2 oz) butter
4 tablespoons golden syrup
30 gm (1 oz) sugar
¼ teaspoon cream of tartar
60 gm (2 oz) flour
½ teaspoons ground ginger
¼ teaspoon cream of tartar

Put the butter, golden syrup and sugar in a pot and heat till melted. Add cream of tartar. Sift flour, soda and ginger together and stir into mixture in pot. Grease a baking tray with butter and then put spoonfulls of mixture in the tray. Form the mixture into a round shape about 4-5 cm (1½-2 in) across. Allow plenty of space between biscuits as they spread during baking. Bake in a moderate oven for about 10 minutes or till golden brown. Allow to cool till pliable and can be lifted off the tray without breaking. Put immediately into small bowls about 10 cm (4 in) in diameter and press round to form a mould. Flute the edges to allow the circles to fit into the bowls. When firm remove from bowl. If the biscuits become too firm to mould replace in oven for a minute to soften. The biscuits may be stored for several days in an airtight container if not to be used immediately. Warming in the oven will allow you to shape them just before filling with fruit.
Makes 6 baskets

Fruit Filling

A number of fruit combinations are suitable using firm fresh colourful fruits, such as pineapple, mango, pawpaw, guava, strawberries, kiwifruit, oranges etc. The following is a particularly attractive and delicious combination.

1 cup sliced kiwifruit
1 cup sliced banana
1 cup sliced mango or peach
1 tablespoon lemon juice
2 teaspoons sugar
½ cup whipped cream

Cut fruit into attractive slices and put into bowl. (The fruit should not contain too much juice). Sprinkle with lemon juice and sugar. Carefully stir with a fork and fill baskets with the mixture. Just before serving top with whipped cream.
Serves 6

Tropical fruit baskets

BRANDIED PAWPAW WHIP

Use as a filling for pavlova or on its own as a dessert.

1 firm pawpaw
½ cup lemon juice
½ cup sugar
1 tablespoon gelatine
2 tablespoons water
1 tablespoon brandy
2 cups whipped cream

Peel and remove the seeds from pawpaw. Mash sufficient to yield 1½ cups. Add lemon juice and sugar. Place in a saucepan and boil for 5 minutes. (This is necessary to remove substance which destroys gelatine). Combine gelatine with water and stir into hot fruit. Reduce fruit to a puree in a blender or by sieving. Add brandy and cool. When partially set, fold in whipped cream. Serve plain or with ice-cream and topped with toasted coconut.
Serves 6

WINE JELLY

A simple but very special dessert. Excellent after a rich main course.

6 cups water
1 cup sugar
15 cloves

Above: Brandied Pawpaw Whip

Below: Wine jelly

5 sticks cinnamon
1 packet lemon jelly powder
2 tablespoons gelatine
1 cup medium sherry
2 tablespoons lemon juice

Bring water, sugar, cloves, and cinnamon sticks to boil. Simmer gently for 10 minutes. Place lemon jelly powder, gelatine, sherry and lemon juice in a bowl. Let stand for 5 minutes. Pour boiling syrup over gelatine mixture and stir well until it is thoroughly dissolved and mixed. Strain. Refrigerate until set. Serve with cream or ice-cream, and fruit of your own choice.
Serves 10-12

Variation
Stir canned or fresh mandarin orange slices into the jelly when it is half set.

Banana orange pie

BANANA ORANGE PIE

Serve this tangy cold dessert with whipped cream or ice-cream. If sweet oranges are used in this recipe, reduce sugar.

1½ cups of orange juice and pulp
½ cup sugar
1½ teaspoons cornflour
2 teaspoons gelatine
1 tablespoon butter

4 medium sized bananas
1 23 cm (9 inch) baked pie shell

Peel and section oranges and strain off juice. Remove all seeds. Put juice in a small saucepan. Mix sugar with cornflour. Add to orange juice and cook until thick and clear. Add remaining orange pulp. Taste to check the mixture is not too acid. A tangy sweet flavour is best. Add a little more sugar at

this time if needed.

Soak gelatine in water. Add to orange mixture and stir until dissolved. Slice bananas to yield approximately 1½ cups. Fold into orange mixture, and refrigerate until cool and slightly firm. Pour into baked pie shell and refrigerate until firm. Serve with whipped cream or cream.

Serves 6

COCONUT PUMPKIN PIE

1 23 cm pie shell
3 eggs well beaten
¾ cup sugar
¼ teaspoon salt
½ teaspoon cinnamon
½ teaspoon nutmeg
½ teaspoon ginger
¼ teaspoon ground cloves
2 cups cooked and sieved pumpkin
2 cups milk
¾ cup grated coconut
1 tablespoon rum

Prepare pie-shell, but do not prick. Beat eggs and sugar together. Add spices, milk, pumpkin, ½ cup coconut, rum. Mix well and pour into 23 cm (9 in) pastry lined pie dish. Sprinkle the top with ¼ cup grated coconut. Bake at 230° C (450° F) for 10 minutes, then reduce heat to 180° C (350° F) and bake for about 20 minutes or until an inserted knife comes out clean. Serve hot or cold with whipped cream or ice cream.
Serves 6-8

SWEET POTATO CUSTARD PIE

A simple dessert pie with a lovely golden creamy filling.

1 23 cm (9 inch) pie shell
1 cup sieved cooked sweet potato
2 cups milk
2 eggs
¾ cup sugar (soft brown)
1 teaspoon cinnamon
¼ teaspoon salt
1 tablespoon lemon juice

Mix cooked sweet potato with milk, ½ cup brown sugar and well beaten eggs. Stir in ½ teaspoon cinnamon, the salt and lemon juice. Mix remaining sugar with ½ teaspoon cinnamon in a separate bowl. Pour custard into the pie-shell. Sprinkle the top with the sugar and cinnamon mixture and bake in oven at 230°C (450°F) for 10 minutes. Reduce heat to 160°C (325°F). Pie will be cooked when the filling puffs up a little and an inserted knife comes out clean (about 15 minutes). Serve hot or

cold with whipped cream or ice cream.

Variation
1. Add ¼ cup brandy to custard mixture
2. Add 1 tablespoon lemon juice
Serves 6-8

CHOCOLATE SWEET POTATO PIE

Using the same basic recipe as the Sweet Potato Custard Pie but with a chocolate topping.

Prepare pie ready for baking but omit sprinkling cinnamon and sugar on top. Bake and partially cool pie.

Prepare the following topping
30 gms (1 oz) dark chocolate
1 teaspoon butter
2 tablespoons boiling water
1 cup sifted icing sugar

Melt dark chocolate with butter in the top of a double boiler, or heavy saucepan. Remove from heat and add boiling water and sifted icing sugar. Beat until smooth and glossy. Pour over warm pie and chill well before serving.
Serves 6

ICED COFFEE TARO DESSERT

¾ cup sugar
2 teaspoons cornflour
pinch of salt
2 teaspoons instant coffee
1 cup milk
1 egg separated
¾ cup water
1 tablespoon lemon juice
4 tablespoons mashed taro
1 tablespoon Kahlua liqueur
whipped cream
toasted almonds

Mix together sugar, cornflour, salt and coffee and slowly stir in milk. Put in a double boiler and stir over boiling water until thickened. Beat egg yolk and add a little hot mixture to it. Then combine with mixture in pot and cook a few minutes. Cool. Put water, taro, and lemon juice in a blender. Blend till very smooth. Combine with milk mixture and stir in Kahlua. Put into freezer tray and freeze till firm. Remove and beat till smooth. Return to tray or freeze in a mould. Serve with whipped cream and garnish with crisp toasted almonds.
Serves 4-6

Iced coffee taro dessert

Tropical Baking

Baking in hot weather can be fraught with problems unless great care is given to the careful storage of ingredients and the use of reliable recipes and techniques of preparation. Ingredients such as baking powder and dried yeast must be kept as fresh as possible.

Always store in airtight tins and keep in a cool place. Keep sugar in a sealed container to prevent the absorption of moisture. Flour, too must be fresh and kept in a covered container so that it is free from moisture. Always sift flour before use.

Cake mixtures containing butter or margarine can often appear very moist in hot weather and the cook is tempted to add extra flour. This moistness is due to the fat becoming soft in the heat so adding extra flour could spoil the recipe. Successful baking depends on following the recipe and practising the techniques.

BASIC GATEAU

Gateau with tropical air

2 20 cm (8 inch) sponge sandwiches (each sponge about 2-3 cm (1-1½ inch) thick
2 cups whipping cream
3 teaspoons liqueur
sliced or diced fresh fruit

Split the sponges in half and put on a flat surface. Whip the cream with the liqueur. Prepare the fruit. Put a layer of fruit on the sponge base, leaving a 2 cm (1 inch) space round the edge. Cover the fruit with a good layer of cream and repeat the process till the last layer of sponge is in place. Flatten the top and proceed to cover the outside with remaining cream and decorate. Keep in refrigerator till served.
Serves 6-8

GATEAU WITH TROPICAL AIR

Making a rich, creamy and spectacular gateau is not as difficult as it may seem. To do this you may use a variety of simple sponge bases filled with fresh fruit and cream. The success of your gateau, however, will depend on following these basic rules:-

1. The layers of sponge must be the same thickness as the fruit and cream filling. To reduce the cost and the richness of the gateau, use a higher proportion of fruit than cream.

2. Always have three layers of sponge, and as you build up the layer and filling, ensure that the top remains flat - do not allow it to become dome-shaped. If necessary trim off the top to keep this flat.

3. Always ensure the whipped cream is slightly sweetened. Add a small amount of liqueur or spirits to enhance the taste and improve the keeping quality of the cream.

Pineapple and kiwifruit gateau

4. Always use an open texture sponge — firmer types of cake make poor gateaux. If possible flavour the sponge with the juice or essence of the fruit being used in the filling.

Some Suggested Combinations

BANANA, PINEAPPLE & RUM

Use the banana cake recipe on page 75 but bake in 20 cm (8 in) sponge tins. Use thick slices of banana soaked in fresh lemon juice and equal quantities of pineapple pieces. Flavour whipped cream with dark rum. Decorate outside with 'fins' of fresh pineapple interspersed with cream rosettes. Decorate top with fresh pineapple and banana, finely diced and soaked in a mixture of equal parts of lemon juice and rum.

Surround with cream rosettes. Use leaves of the pineapple top to make the appearance more spectacular.

PINEAPPLE, COCONUT & KIWIFRUIT

Use the lolo coconut cake recipe on page 75 without getting to the topping stage. Use a 20 cm (8 in) round or square cake tin. Use slices of kiwifruit, peeled, and cream flavoured with either one of the new coconut-based liqueurs or a light white rum. Smooth the outside with cream and coat with toasted grated coconut. Top all over with thinly slice kiwifruit. Edge with tiny cream rosettes.

Variation

Use alternate slices of kiwifruit and pineapple

ORANGE & MANGO

Use a plain vanilla sponge with grated orange rind added. The filling should be of equal quantities of orange segments and chunks of mango. Cream is best flavoured with an orange-based liqueur such as Curacao, Cointreau, or Grand Marnier. Decorate outside with smoothed cream on which whole slices of peeled oranges are laid. Top with finely sliced mango and edge with large piped rosettes capped with finely chopped nuts.

CHOCOLATE PAWPAW & PASSIONFRUIT

For those who do not like alcohol here is a delicious alternative. Make the chocolate cake on page 75 and fill with whipped cream flavoured with 2 tablespoons of fresh passionfruit juice and 1 tablespoon of icing sugar. Decorate the outside with browned almonds or grated dark dessert chocolate. Pipe large rosettes round the edge and cap with round mint chocolates cut in half with a hot knife.

LOLO COCONUT CAKE

2 eggs
1 cup sugar
1 teaspoon vanilla
1 cup flour
1 teaspoon baking powder
¼ teaspoon salt
½ cup very thick coconut cream

Topping
1 cup freshly grated coconut
3 tablespoons melted butter
5 tablespoons brown sugar

Beat eggs. Gradually add sugar and continue beating until mixture is thick and light. Add vanilla. Sift flour, baking powder and salt together. Slowly add to egg mixture, mixing well after each addition. Heat coconut cream to boiling point but do not allow to boil. Fold into the mixture.

Bake in a greased and floured 20 cm (8 in) square tin, in a 180º C (350º F) oven for 40-50 minutes. The cake will spring back when pressed with the finger and will be a golden brown colour when done. Prepare topping by mixing freshly grated coconut, melted butter and brown sugar. Spread evenly over hot cake and place under griller for 3-4 minutes or until brown. This must be watched closely so it does not burn. Leave in tin to cool.

BANANA CAKE

120 gms (4 oz) butter or margarine
½ cup castor sugar
2 eggs
1½ cups self-raising flour
(or 1½ cups plain flour & 2½ teaspoons baking powder)
½ teaspoon salt
1 teaspoon vanilla
2 tablespoons milk
3 small or 2 large bananas

Cream margarine or butter and sugar together. Beat in eggs. Sift together self-raising flour, or plain flour and baking powder, and salt. Alternately fold in flour and milk.

Lolo coconut cake

Mash bananas and fold into cake mixture.
Place in a greased 20 cm (8 in) cake tin, and bake in a 180ºC (350ºF) oven for 30-35 minutes.

RUM CHOCOLATE CAKE

½ cup water
½ cup cocoa
1½ teaspoons bicarbonate soda
⅔ cup of butter
1¾ cups sugar
2 eggs
1 teaspoon vanilla
2 teaspoons vinegar & 1 cup milk
(or 1 cup sour cream or sour milk)
2 cups flour
½ cup cornflour
½ teaspoon salt

Heat water, cocoa and bicarbonate soda over low heat, stirring until smooth paste has formed. Remove from heat and allow to cool. Beat butter with sugar until light and fluffy. Beat in eggs and vanilla. Add vinegar to milk, stir and allow to stand for 5 minutes or use sour milk or cream.
Sift flour with cornflour and salt.

Beat cool chocolate into butter mixture and then alternately add sour milk and dry ingredients, beating well after each addition.
Pour into two 20 cm (8in) cake tins which have been lined, greased and floured. Bake in a 180º C (350º F) oven for 30-40 minutes. When done, remove from oven and leave in tin for 5 minutes before turning out onto cake rack.
Ice with the following rum flavoured chocolate frosting.

Chocolate Rum Frosting

¼ cup cocoa
2 cups icing sugar
1 egg
⅔ cup butter
¼ cup milk
2 teaspoons rum
½ teaspoon vanilla essence

Sift cocoa with icing sugar. Thoroughly blend in egg and butter. Add sugar mixture and milk alternately, beating well after each addition. Flavour with rum and vanilla.

Left: Ripe breadfruit cake with ginger. Above: Rum chocolate cake

RIPE BREADFRUIT CAKE
(with ginger)

This cake has a moist texture similar to a Madeira cake and a delicious, unique flavour.

½ cup butter or margarine
1½ cups sugar
2 eggs
½ teaspoon vanilla
1 teaspoon baking powder
1 teaspoon baking soda
2 cups flour
1 cup mashed ripe breadfruit
¼ cup milk

Beat butter and sugar till creamy, add vanilla and beat in eggs, one at a time. Sift flour and baking powder. Mix baking soda with milk. Mix the breadfruit with the butter, sugar, egg, and baking soda. Stir well and put mixture in a well greased tin. Bake for about 45 minutes at 160ºC (325ºF) or till cooked.

Variation

Add ½ cup of chopped crystallized ginger to mixture and decorate the top of the cake with slices of crystallized ginger.

GINGER MANGO SHORTCAKE

The base for this delicious dessert is Scottish shortbread. This biscuit base has many uses. It makes a crisp and firm shell for cheesecakes and cream pies, as well as biscuits and shortcake. The pastry can be flavoured with ginger or grated orange or lemon rind.

Basic Shortcake

125 gms (4 oz) sugar
220 gms (7 oz) butter
2 teaspoons fresh crushed ginger
(or ½ teaspoon dried, or 2 teaspoons grated orange or lemon rind)
250 gms (8 oz) plain flour
60 gms (2 oz) cornflour
(or rice flour)
¼ teaspoon salt

Cut the butter into small pieces and beat into sugar. Add the ginger or grated rind. Sift the dry ingredients and work into the butter mixture using a knife or pastry blender. Keep the mixture cool. Form into a ball, wrap in greaseproof paper and place in the refrigerator for 30 minutes. Flatten out the pastry till 1 cm (½ inch) thick and cut into rounds using a

Ginger mango shortcake

10 cm (4 in) biscuit cutter. Place on a greased baking tray. This should provide 12 rounds. Prick carefully with a fork. Pre-heat the oven to 230ºC (450ºF) and cook for 5 minutes. Then turn down to 180ºC (350ºF) and cook for up to 30 minutes more. Do not leave too long - the shortcake will be ready when it turns a light golden colour. It burns very quickly. Leave to cool and store in an airtight tin.

Filling
1 cup whipped cream
2 teaspoons rum, brandy or passion-fruit juice
thin slices of poached mango (see page 66)

Add the flavouring to the cream and whip. Place mango slices on top of shortcake rounds. Pipe around the edge with cream. Top with a second shortcake round which may be cut in half to make 'wings'. Decorate with cream and a piece of cherry.

Alternative: kiwifruit with orange liqueur-flavoured cream or pineapple with kirsch flavoured cream, both using orange rind in the shortcake base.
A useful dessert for last minute entertaining.
Serves 6

FRUIT MUFFINS

Perfect for breakfast or afternoon tea and coffee. These muffins may be made using most types of tropical fruit finely chopped.

2 cups plain flour
3 beaten eggs
¾ cup castor sugar
¼ teaspoon salt
300 ml (½ pint) milk
3 tablespoons melted butter
500 gms (1 lb) guava, mango, pineapple or ripe cherries cut up and lightly poached in sugar syrup (page 64)

Combine the flour, eggs and ½ cup sugar, then add the salt. Beat thoroughly, add milk and continue beating until smooth. Fold in the melted butter. Drain poached fruit (if using Brazil cherries, rinse, and dry on paper). Add to the mixture. Butter individual patty tins thoroughly and pour in the mixture. Bake in a moderately hot oven 200ºC (400ºF) for 30-40 minutes until the muffins have risen and are golden brown. Allow to cool and sprinkle with remaining sugar.
Makes about 24 muffins

PLAIN SCONES

A simple and basic scone mixture to which variations may be added.

2 cups flour
3 teaspoons baking powder
1 teaspoon salt
⅓ cup margarine or butter
⅔ cup milk

Measure and sift flour, baking powder and salt in a bowl. Using two knives cut in margarine or butter until a coarse meal-like consistency is reached. Measure milk, slowly add this to the mixture, while stirring with a fork. Add milk only to dry areas. Reserve the last two tablespoons. Check the consistency before adding more. The dough should be soft, pliable and non-sticky.
Form into a ball. Place on a slightly floured board, and knead half a dozen times. Roll out scones till 1 cm (½ in) thick. Cut into rounds using a 5 cm (2 in) biscuit cutter. Place on an ungreased baking sheet and bake in a 220ºC (425ºF) oven for 12-15 minutes. They will be done when a light golden brown with raised layered sides.

Variations
Coconut Scones
Substitute coconut cream for milk in plain scones.

Herb Scones
Add 1 teaspoon mixed herbs and ¼ teaspoon dried mustard to flour mixture in plain scones.

Health Scones
Replace white flour with 1¾ cups wholemeal and ¼ cup of bran or wheat germ.

BANANA SCONES

Delicious plain or with butter. Quick and easy to make for afternoon tea.

2 cups flour
½ teaspoon salt
3 teaspoons baking powder
¼ cup sugar
2 tablespoons butter melted
½ cup mashed banana
1 egg
2 tablespoons milk

Sift flour, salt, baking powder and sugar together. Melt butter. Beat banana, butter, egg and milk together. Make a hollow in the flour mixture. Pour liquid in and mix with a fork. Stir until there are no areas of flour left. Drop onto a greased baking sheet using two spoons. Bake in 200ºC (400ºF) oven.
Makes 18 scones

Variation: Breadfruit Scones
Prepare banana scones, folding ½ cup sultanas into dry ingredients and substituting ½ cup cooked grated breadfruit for banana. Increase milk to ½ cup plus 2 tablespoons. Bake as directed for banana scones.

PUMPKIN SCONES

1 tablespoon margarine or butter
½ cup sugar
1 tablespoon hot water
1 egg
1 cup cold cooked sieved pumpkin
3 teaspoons baking powder
2 cups flour
½ teaspoon salt

Blend margarine or butter and sugar with hot water. Beat in egg and cold pumpkin. Sift and stir in baking powder, flour, salt. Mix until no dry areas are left. Using two spoons, drop on a greased biscuit tray. Bake in a 200ºC (400ºF) oven for 12-15 minutes.
Makes 16 scones

Variation
Add ½ teaspoon cinnamon, ¼ teaspoon grated nutmeg to flour.

COCONUT FRUIT SCONES

2 cups flour
½ teaspoon salt
3 teaspoons baking powder
¼ cup margarine or butter
¼ cup sugar
¾ cup dried mixed fruit
(or chopped dried pawpaw, banana or pineapple)
1 egg
⅓ cup milk
1 cup freshly grated coconut

Sift flour, salt and baking powder together. Work margarine or butter into mixture, using two knives as directed in basic plain scones. Mix in sugar and dried mixed fruit. Beat egg, milk and coconut together. Slowly add to flour mixture until no dry areas are left and a soft non-

Fruit muffins, banana scones and guava jelly

79

Meringues with Creme de Menthe filling.

sticky dough is achieved. It may not be necessary to use all the liquid. Turn out on to floured board, knead half a dozen times. Pat or roll out dough until it is 1½ cm (½ in) thick. Cut into rounds using a floured 5 cm (2in) biscuit cutter. Place on a greased baking sheet and bake in a 220°C (425°F) oven for 12-15 minutes or until risen and golden brown. Place on a wired rack to cool.

Makes 24 scones

TROPICAL MERINGUES

Equally good with coffee or as a dessert.

4 egg whites
1¾ cups sugar
2 teaspoons lemon juice or vinegar
2 tablespoons boiling water

Separate egg whites. Put in a bowl and stir in the sugar and lemon juice. Leave for at least 2 hours, stirring occasionally. During this time the sugar partly dissolves. Place the bowl over hot water and beat. When the mixture starts to froth, add the boiling water, whilst beating. Continue beating till the mixture forms peaks that stand up. Grease a tray with butter and pipe or spoon the mixture onto the tray to make individual meringues.

Alternatively, to make a Pavlova, grease a piece of butter paper and spoon all the mixture into a round shape This should be about 23 cm (9 in) in diameter, and about 4 cm (1½ in) deep. Raise the top edges by piping or spooning around extra mixture.

Bake in a cool oven till dry, at 100°C (200°F). The meringues are cooked when they lift easily off the tray. Store in air-tight containers.

Fill the centres of the meringues with whipped cream flavoured with vanilla, passionfruit or a liqueur such as Creme de Menthe.

Makes about 3 dozen meringues.

Meringue mixture should be consistency as shown.

Pavlova Fillings

1. Brandied pawpaw whip (p.70)
2. Whipped cream flavoured with rum or Tia Maria liqueur and sprinkled with chocolate chips.
3. Whipped cream mixed with crystallized ginger.
4. Chopped fruit mixed with whipped cream

Accompaniments

Many simple dishes are enhanced by an attractive accompaniment.

Tropical fruit jellies and chutneys go well with hot and cold meals. A curry served with a variety of fresh vegetable chutneys becomes a highlight of the menu and cold meats are often improved when served with a delicious preserve. Chutneys are particularly useful as a flavour booster in stews and casseroles.

In this chapter, we introduce some simple but reliable recipes for jams, jellies, pickles and chutneys.

Most tropical fruits and vegetables make excellent jams, jellies, pickles and chutneys, which can be used in a variety of ways.

Hints About Making and Storing Preserves

Jams and Jellies are more difficult to store in hot climates but in any climate it is a good idea to follow these rules if you want your preserves to last.

1. Clean glass jars must be sterilized by heating in an oven at 120°C (250°F).

2. The boiling jams or jellies should be poured into the hot jars and covered with a clean cloth. When partly cooled, seal with boiling wax and then cover with greaseproof paper or damp cellophane and a rubber band.

3. Jars should be stored in a cool, airy cupboard.

4. Dust jars regularly to prevent mould forming on the lids or paper covers.

JELLIES

Excellent jellies can be made from these fruits: guava, mango, Tahitian apple (*Spondias dulcis*), Brazil cherry (*Eugenia michelli*), Java cherry (*Flacourtca inermis*), lemons, limes, cumquats, passionfruit, rosella (*Hibiscus sabdariffa*).

BASIC JELLY

Wash and remove stalks and blemishes from half-ripe fruit. Slice large fruits. Include the seeds with the flesh. Put fruit in a large pot and add sufficient water to half cover. Bring to the boil and cook till fruit is soft and mushy. Strain through a jelly bag made of linen, nylon or double butter muslin.(Do not squeeze bag). For high acid fruits — mango, Tahitian apple, red currants, sour green or cooking apples, Java cherry, Brazil cherry, and citrus — add 1 cup sugar to every cup of juice.

For low acid fruits — guava, passionfruit, rosella and kiwifruit, use ¾ cup of fruit juice and ¼ cup lemon juice to 1 cup sugar. Stir well until sugar is dissolved and mixture boils. The mixture should not be allowed to boil before the sugar has dissolved.

Put 6 cups of juice in a pan with 6 cups of sugar. Boil rapidly till a skin forms when gently pushed with finger. Remove white scum as it forms during the cooking. It is important to cook jelly in small quantities; six cups is the maximum amount for successful boiling.

Brazil Cherry
A pinkish yellow colour. Contains plenty of pectin and sets easily. Goes well with lamb.

Java Cherry
Makes one of the best tropical jellies. It has a deep red colour and a fine tart flavour. Excellent as a spread or with meats. (Similar to red currant jelly.)

Guava

Gives a light red juice with a distinctive flavour. Guavas do not contain sufficient acid to set well. Lemon juice or other acid fruit must be included in the recipe. If the ripening season has been very wet, reduce the amount of water when boiling.

Passionfruit

Remove pulp from fruit, cut up skins, just cover with water and boil for about half an hour. Strain off water and add to pulp. Boil for a few minutes and then strain. For a more tart flavour, add 1 tablespoon of lemon juice to 1 cup of passion-fruit.

Mango

Use green or half-ripe fruits. Peel and cut in slices remove the stones from green mangoes as they have a bitter flavour. Mango juice contains plenty of pectin. The jelly has a clear light yellow colour with an acid flavour. Suitable for spreads or meats. May be flavoured with mint or lemon.

FRUIT SALAD JAM

8 Tahitian apples
(or green mangoes or cooking apples)
2 cups sliced banana
2 cups cubed pineapple
2 cups cubed pawpaw
½ cup passionfruit pulp
1 orange, grated rind
2 tablespoons lemon juice

Wash apples or mangoes, cut up (leave skin on apples but peel mangoes). Just cover with water and boil till soft. Strain in a cloth. Reserve the juice and put in large pan. Add the cut-up fruit, pulp, grated rind and lemon juice. Bring to the boil and cook 5 minutes. Remove and measure the fruit and liquid. Add 1 cup of sugar to every cup of fruit and juice. Boil till

From left: Pickled chillies, Guava jelly, Pickled watermelon, Oriental vegetable pickle, Cumquat marmalade, Guava jelly, Mango chutney

testing a small amount in a saucer shows that the jam will set.

GUAVA JAM

guavas
lemon juice
sugar

Prepare guavas as for jelly. Cook till soft and then rub through a sieve. Measure the pulp and add 1 cup of sugar to every cup of pulp and lemon juice. Boil till mixture

sets. Stir frequently to prevent sticking to pan.

Variation

Peel and seed half-ripe guavas. Cover the pulp and skins with water and boil till soft. Strain in a cloth and reserve the juice. Cut the shells into small strips or squares. Measure the juice and add 1 cup of cut-up fruit to 1 cup of juice. Boil for a few minutes and then add 1 cup of sugar and 1 tablespoon

CITRUS MARMALADE

1 large grapefruit
2 oranges
8 cumquats
4 limes
water
sugar

Any of these fruits may be substituted for each other. However, the best marmalade is made from fruits used in equal proportions. Cut grapefruit and oranges into quarters, remove seeds and slice finely. Cut cumquats in half, seed and slice. Peel limes and slice the inner flesh. Place fruit in a bowl and cover with water. Leave overnight. Boil till the skins are tender, cool and measure in cups. Add 1 cup of sugar to each cup of pulp, Boil till testing a small amount in a saucer shows that jam will set.

MANGO CHUTNEY

This moderately hot chutney goes well with curries and cold meats

2.5 kg (5 lb) mangoes
⅓ cup salt
8 cups water
3 tablespoons pickling spice
4-5 small red chillies, or 2 large
3 tablespoons chopped green ginger
2½ cups vinegar
4 cups sugar

Choose half-ripe mangoes with pale yellow firm flesh. Peel and slice. Put in a bowl and soak overnight in salted water. Drain well. Prepare a cloth bag and in this put the three tablespoons of pickling spice, ginger and chopped seeded chillies. Tie up and put in the vinegar and boil for 2-3 minutes. Add sugar and stir till dissolved then add the mangoes.Bring to the boil and simmer till the mangoes are easily pierced with a fork. When done the syrup should be clear and the mangoes partly

lemon juice to each cup of cooked fruit. Boil till testing a little in a saucer shows jam will set.

MANGO JAM

12 mangoes
water
lemon juice
sugar
almonds

almond essence (optional)

Peel half-ripe mangoes, slice and measure in cups. Add ¾ cup of water and ¼ cup of lemon juice to each cup of fruit. Place in a saucepan and cook till just soft. Measure. Add 1 cup of sugar to each cup of fruit pulp. Half a cup of peeled and chopped almonds and 2 teaspoons of almond essence may be included to give more flavour. Boil till jam sets.

transparent. The pieces should remain whole and not become soft and mushy. Remove from heat, take out the spice bag and pack mangoes into sterile jars. Seal with airtight lids.

HOT SPICY TOMATO CHUTNEY

A chutney that goes well with pilau and vegetable curry as well as cold meats.

2 tablespoons oil
½ teaspoon cumin seed
½ teaspoon fenugreek seed
½ teaspoon mustard seed
1 clove garlic
1 tablspooon chopped green ginger
500 gms (1 lb) tomatoes
½ teaspoon turmeric
salt to taste
1 teaspoon tamarind
(or teaspoon lemon juice)
1 tablespoon water
2 tablespoons chopped coriander leaves or parsley

Heat oil in a saucepan and add spices. Saute for a few minutes. Crush garlic and ginger, add to spices and saute a futher few minutes. Peel fresh tomatoes, chop and add to spices. Alternatively use the same quantity of canned tomatoes. Season with turmeric and salt to taste. Mix tamarind or lemon juice with water. Chop coriander leaves finely and add with tamarind to other ingredients and cook for 10-12 minutes over low heat. Pour into sterilised jars and seal. Can be used straight away. Store any remainder in refrigerator.

Variation
1 medium onion
2 teaspoons lemon juice

Add chopped onion to garlic and ginger. Replace tamarind with lemon juice.

Pacific Islands Cookbook

HOT SWEET PINEAPPLE CHUTNEY

A delicious accompaniment to pork and ham.

2.5 kg (5 lb) peeled pineapple
2 cups sugar
3 cups vinegar
2 tablespoons chopped green ginger
3 cloves garlic
2 onions
2 tablespoons salt
1 grated lemon rind
1 cinnamon stick
2 red chillies

Cut the pineapple into cubes and put in a large pan. Add sugar, vinegar, finely chopped ginger, crushed garlic, chopped onions, salt, grated lemon rind, cinnamon and the chopped seeded chillies. Bring to the boil and cook slowly till mixture thickens. Put into sterile jars and seal.

Variations
½ cup chopped almonds
1 cup sultanas
These can be added towards the end of cooking.

2 kg (4 lbs) pineapple
½ kg (1 lb) diced watermelon
Use less pineapple and make up the difference with diced watermelon. The pink and yellow fruit combination makes a very pretty chutney.

HOT SPICY LIME PICKLE

1 kg (2 lb) limes
4 tablespoons salt
1 teaspoon turmeric
2 teaspoons garam masala
(or curry powder)
1-2 teaspoons chilli powder
2-3 green chillies

Cut limes into eighths. Mix together spices, salt and chopped chillies. Mix well with limes and

then put in a screw-topped jar and cover. Keep in a warm place for a week, shaking the jar every day. The pickle is ready to use when the lime skins become soft.

Variation
Add ½ cup sugar to the basic recipe. Serve with curries.

PLAIN LIME PICKLE

6 limes
6 tablespoons salt
3 teaspoons turmeric
lime juice

Cut limes in quarters almost to the base. Fill the centres with a mixture of salt and turmeric. Pack into jars, cover with lime juice. Seal and leave in warm place. Shake daily. It will be ready to use when the skins are soft.
Delicious served with fish dishes.

ORIENTAL VEGETABLE PICKLE

250 gms (½ lb) carrots or watermelon
250 gms (½ lb) white radish
500 gms (1 lb) cucumbers
2 cups water
3 cups sugar
¼ cup salt
2 cups vinegar

Peel and thinly slice carrots and radishes. Cut cucumbers and melon into pieces about 5 cm (2 in) long. Pack vegetables into clean jars. Put salt, sugar, water and vinegar in a saucepan and bring to the boil. Cool and fill jars making sure that the vegetables are completely covered. Cover and keep in a cool place for three days before using. Store in a refrigerator.
Serve as an accompaniment to cold meat and sweet and sour dishes.

Variation
Use half cucumber and half water melon slices.

FRESH CUCUMBER PICKLE

2 medium cucumbers
2-3 teaspoons salt
French dressing or lemon juice
2 teaspoons chopped chives or dill

Peel cucumbers and thinly slice. Sprinkle with salt and leave to drain for 1-2 hours. Marinate in a little French dressing, or with lemon juice mixed with chives or dill. Serve with fish or egg dishes.

FRESH GREEN PAWPAW PICKLE

Delicious with cold meats and salads

1 medium green pawpaw
1 tablespoon lemon juice
2 teaspoons salt
1 teaspoon grated green ginger
black pepper
1 chopped mild red chilli

Peel and remove seeds from a green pawpaw. Shred the flesh in a coarse grater. Put in a bowl and mix in lemon juice, salt and pepper chillie and green ginger.

Variation
½ cup grated carrot
or finely chopped capsicum.

FRUIT KETCHUP

Green mangoes, guava, tomatoes, water to make 5 cups fruit puree
1 cup vinegar
1 cup sugar
1 tablespoon salt
1 teaspoon ground allspice
1 teaspoon mixed spice
1 teaspoon cinnamon
4 cloves
1 large onion
3 cloves garlic
1 tablespoon chopped green ginger
2-3 chillies
1 lemon or lime rind grated

Peel chosen fruit, chop up and place in a saucepan with sufficient water to cover. Cook till soft and then puree or sieve.
To every 5 cups of puree add the ingredients as listed. The onion should be finely chopped or grated and the garlic and ginger crushed to a pulp. Seed and then chop the chillies. Finely grate the skin of the lemon or lime. The mixture should be cooked over medium heat for about 30 minutes. Stir frequently to avoid sticking. If too thick, add a little boiling water. Pour into sterile bottles and seal with a crown cap or cork.
Note: The preparation of this sauce can be speeded up by putting ginger, garlic, onion and chillies in the blender. This sauce is very good served with hot or cold meats.

FRESH TOMATO SAUCE

An easy-to-make and versatile sauce. Much nicer than commercial tomato sauce.

1½ tablespoons oil
1 medium onion
1 cup peeled and chopped tomatoes (or canned tomatoes)
1 cup stock, or water
½ teaspoon sugar
½ teaspoon salt
1 teaspoon chopped fresh basil
2 teaspoons cornflour
¼ cup water

Saute chopped onion in oil and then add tomatoes, stock, sugar, salt and basil. Simmer for about 10 minutes. If desired, thicken with cornflour mixed with ¼ cup water. Cook for a few minutes before serving.
Note: Tomato puree, or paste, may be used in place of tomatoes but does not give quite as good a flavour. Use 1 tablespoon of paste with 1 cup of water, ½ cup puree with ½ cup water.
Makes 2 cups of sauce

COCONUT CREAM SAUCE (Miti)

Use with vegetables and fish

1 grated coconut
1 small lemon
1-2 chillies
2 tablespoons chopped onion
salt

Mix all ingredients together and leave for several hours. Squeeze out the coconut cream using hands or put in butter muslin cloth and squeeze. Strain and serve.

CHILLI WINE or VINEGAR

small hot chillies
white vinegar, gin or dry sherry

Clean the chillies and remove stalks. Pack into bottles and then cover with vinegar, gin or dry sherry. Seal bottles and leave for several months. Use a few drops in soups, stews or tomato dishes.

FRESH CHILLI TOMATO SAUCE

Hot and spicy

½ cup chillies
½ cup oil
1 clove garlic
1 tablespoon chopped parsley
½ cup peanut butter
6 medium tomatoes
salt and pepper

Wash chillies, cut in half and remove seeds. Put in a jar and cover with oil. Leave for several days. Crush chillies and garlic to a paste (this is best done in the blender). Add chopped parsley, peanut butter and peeled chopped tomatoes. Season with salt and pepper, and blend or pound.
Serve with steak, kebabs, savoury rice. This sauce keeps well in the refrigerator.
Makes 2 cups

Drinks

Tropical fruits are particularly suited to refreshing drinks and cocktails. Attractively served, they are an essential part of tropical meals and entertainment. With the wide range of fruits now available in many countries, any number of delicious combinations are possible to which tea, alcohol and other flavourings can be added.

Nowadays, more and more people are requesting non-alcoholic punches and long drinks at parties. Punches have a stronger flavour than fruit squashes or -ades. Serve in similar glasses allowing 120-150 ml (4-5 fluid oz) per person. Long drinks, like orange or lemonade, are poured into large glasses allowing 1 cup (250 ml or 8 oz) per serving.

All cold drinks must be well chilled. Serve with ice cubes or crushed ice and a garnish. Colourful garnishes such as, maraschino cherries, watermelon or pawpaw balls or cubes, sliced orange, lime, lemon or cucumber or pineapple, sprigs or leaves of mint, lemon balm, peppermint or blue borage flowers with a little leaf, add flavour and colour. Pieces of fruit may be put on a tooth pick, skewer, frozen in ice cubes or floated on top of the drink.

The preparation of fruit drinks is simplified if some of the basic ingredients, such as syrups, "teas", citric acid and frozen cubes of lemon or lime juice, are kept on hand.

SYRUP

2 cups sugar
4 cups water
1 teaspoon citric acid
rind (zest) of one large lemon

Put all ingredients in a pot and bring to boil. Simmer 5 minutes, strain and pour into sterile bottles, seal and store in a cool place.

Use this syrup to flavour long drinks and punches. To make zest, peel off thin outer layer of lemon skin with a sharp potato peeler.

For low-calorie drinks, replace all or part of the sugar with an artificial sweetener. Most sweeteners give the equivalent amount needed to replace one teaspoon of sugar.

Note: There are about 56 teaspoons of sugar in one cup.

Acid Flavours

All fruit drinks benefit from the addition of some acid flavour. Fresh lemon or lime juice are the best ingredients. For a regular supply, freeze juice in ice cube trays and store in plastic bags. The acidity of 1 cup of lemon juice may be replaced by 1 teaspoon of citric acid dissolved in 1 cup of warm water.

Teas made from spices, herbs and tea leaves impart a subtle flavour to many punches and long drinks.

SPICED TEA

4 cups water
2 teaspoons chopped green ginger
8 whole cloves
5 cm (2 in) piece cinnamon

Put all together in a pot and simmer for five minutes. Cool and strain. Spiced tea may be used in punches and drinks with a rum base.

LEMON LEAF TEA

12 lemon leaves
4 cups water

Crush leaves in the hand. Add water and bring to the boil. Remove from heat and cool. Strain. Use this tea as a base for any fruit drink, or take as a hot or chilled drink, with or without sugar.

At right: Sunset punch

SUNSET PUNCH

1.5 kg (3 lb) watermelon

Cut watermelon in half and cut out the red flesh, including 1 cm (½ inch) white rind. Make 1 cup of watermelon balls (or dice into small cubes). Remove seeds from remaining flesh and put in a blender or mash well. Strain pulp through a wire strainer.

2 cups watermelon juice
2 cups unsweetened pineapple juice
¼ cup of lemon or lime juice
4 cups soda water
syrup to taste
1 cup watermelon balls
½ cup pineapple wedges
mint leaves

Mix fruit juices and fruit. Chill well. Just before serving add soda water and a little syrup if necessary. Pour into punch glasses and garnish with watermelon balls and pineapple wedges or segments of fruit.
Makes 12-18 punch glasses

Long Drinks

ORANGE PASSION-FRUIT—ADE

1 cup fresh passionfruit juice
½ cup orange juice
¼ cup lemon or lime juice
2 cups water or soda water
syrup to taste
ice
orange slices

Mix fruit juices together and add syrup to taste. The amount of syrup you need will depend on the passionfruit flavour. Tropical fruits are generally more tart than temperate kinds. Add cold water or soda water, serve in long glasses garnished with a slice of orange
Makes 4-5 large glasses

PLANTERS PINEAPPLE PUNCH

This simple and refreshing drink comes from the plantations of Fiji. A good way to use the left overs of fresh pineapple.

Several pineapple skins and cores
4 lemon leaves to each pineapple skin
water to cover skins

Put the pineapple skins in a pot with lemon leaves. Cover with water. Bring to the boil and simmer 10 minutes. Leave to cool in pot. Strain and chill. Pour into a jug and serve with ice cubes and few cubes of pineapple. Add a little lemon juice or syrup to taste.

MANGO PAWPAW PUNCH

1 cup syrup
1 cup spiced tea
½ cup lemon juice
1½ cups mango juice
3 cups tea
2 cups soda water
slices of lime or lemon
slices of mango and pawpaw

Mix all ingredients except the soda water. Chill well. Put in a bowl and add fruit slices. Add soda water just before serving.
Note: For a more acid flavour, increase lemon juice to ¾ cup.
Makes 16-20 punch glasses

PINEAPPLE LEMON PUNCH

8 cups tea
1 cup lemon juice
4 cups pineapple juice (unsweetened)
1 cup syrup
1 sliced lemon or lime
4 slices pineapple cut into wedges
4 sprigs mint
ice
large bottle ginger ale

Put tea, lemon juice, pineapple juice and syrup in a jug and chill well. Serve in a punch bowl with plenty of ice, slices of lemon, pineapple pieces and sprigs of mint. Leave covered for an hour or so to allow flavours to develop. Add chilled ginger ale just before serving.
Note: If sweetened pineapple juice is used omit syrup and add an extra cup of juice.
Makes about 30 punch glasses

GREEN COCONUT COOLER

Select half-mature green nuts. Remove the husk, leaving a section on the base. Cut this flat so that the nut will stand upright. Chill the nuts. To serve, make holes through two eyes and insert a straw in one eye, or cut off the top and serve with a straw. A delicious and refreshing drink.

Green coconut cooler

SOURSOP COOLER

Soursop has a distinct and refreshing flavour which lends itself ideally to cool drinks.

Take one medium ripe soursop about 1 kg (2 lbs).
Peel and strain by pushing through a wire strainer. Measure juice and freeze any surplus.

3 cups soursop juice
¼ cup lemon juice
2-3 cups water
(or watermelon juice)
syrup to taste

Mix fruit juices, water and syrup. Chill. Serve garnished with slices of lime or watermelon balls. (Watermelon juice can replace water.)

Drinks With Alcohol

The flavour of fruit punch is often improved by adding a little sherry, port, rum, brandy or wine.
As a general rule add sherry to grapefruit juice; port to watermelon; rum to spice-flavoured punches and pineapple; brandy to orange, passionfruit, mango or pawpaw; and white wine to any fruit-based punch.

WINE & FRUIT PUNCH

This punch makes a refreshing drink for hot weather parties.

1 cup lemon or lime juice
1 cup pineapple juice
1 cup guava juice
1 orange
1 lime or small lemon
cucumber slices
mint leaves
3 bottles chilled dry white wine
syrup
ice cubes

Mix fruit juices with sliced fruit, 6 slices of cucumber and a few sprigs of mint. Chill for several hours. Just before serving add white wine and 12-18 ice cubes. Test flavour and add syrup if needed.

Variation
Replace guava juice with extra pineaple juice.
Makes 40-50 punch glasses.

MANGO CUP

3 cups mango juice
3 tablespoons lime or lemon juice
1 teaspoon grated lime or lemon rind
½ cup brandy
1 bottle semi-sweet sparkling wine
ice cubes
maraschino cherries

Mix mango, lemon juice and rind and brandy. Chill. Just before serving add wine and ice cubes. Garnish with a cherry on a tooth pick.
Serves 10-12 punch glasses.

JAMAICAN PUNCH

½ cup spiced tea
½ cup lime or lemon juice
2 cups orange juice
1 lime or lemon sliced
1 750 ml (26 oz) bottle dark or light rum
1 750 ml (26oz) bottle chilled ginger ale
2 cups syrup or to taste

Mix all ingredients except ginger ale. Chill well. Just before serving add ginger ale.
Makes 20-25 punch glasses

Pineapple and lemon punch

Essentials of Tropical Cooking

SPICES

Spices are an essential part of many tropical dishes. To get the best results from these wonderfully aromatic and flavoursome additions to your cooking depends on knowing how to select, prepare, use, and store them.

Preparation of Spices

When bought fresh always wash and then dry in the sun or a warm oven till crisp. Store in airtight containers. For long storage keep in the refrigerator or deep freeze. Grind spices using a spice or coffee grinder. Always clean the grinder thoroughly with a little methylated spirits on a piece of cotton wool to remove flavours.

When using whole spices like cloves and cinnamon sticks, bruise the spices with a heavy spoon to release the flavour. In curries, pilaus and similar dishes, spices are sauteed in oil, ghee or butter at a low to medium heat to develop the flavours. Care must be taken not to overheat the oil or ghee as this will spoil the spices.

Large pieces of whole spice may be removed before serving to improve the appearance of the dish. Smaller spices like cardamom seeds or cumin may be left in dishes.

Masalas

A masala is a basic mixture of spices which varies greatly according to individual tastes and to the different regions of India. When turmeric is added it then becomes known as curry (or kari) powder. A simple masala would be coriander and peppercorn, ground and blended, using about 3 times as much coriander as black pepper. Other masalas may be coriander, fenugreek, and mustard seed; or coriander, peppercorn, cinnamon, cumin, and fennel.
For example -

3 tablespoons coriander seeds
1 tablespoon cumin
1 tablespoon black pepper
1 tablespoon mustard seed
1 tablespoon cloves
1 tablespoon turmeric
1 tablespoon ground ginger
(or freshly crushed ginger root)

For this masala, grind whole dry spices and add turmeric at end.

GARAM MASALA

Garam masala is a fragrant strong mixture which is suitable for meat, fried and braised food.

ingredients for Garam Masala
continued on page 92

SPICES & HERBS (opposite)

1. **Garlic**
2. **Turmeric**
3. **Lime**
4. **Cinnamon sticks**
5. **Cloves**
6. **Nutmeg**
7. **Fennel seeds**
8. **Cardamoms**
9. **Chillies**
10. **Capsicums**
11. **Black peppercorns**
12. **Star anise**
13. **Cumin**
14. **Black mustard**
15. **Chilli powder**
16. **Root ginger**
17. **Mint**
18. **Coriander**

GARAM MASALA

6 tablespoons black peppercorns
5 tablespoons caraway seeds
1¾ tablespoons cinnamon stick
6 tablespoons dried coriander
1¾ tablespoons cloves
1½ tablespoons cardamom seeds

Prepare as directed under preparation of masala. Grind and blend. Store in airtight jar.

YOGHURT

This essential ingredient of many Asian dishes may be easily prepared at home.

600 ml (1 pint) milk
2 tablespoons dried skim milk
4 tablespoons commercial or home-made yoghurt

Heat milk till just below boiling point or until it is frothy, but not boiling. Cool to blood heat. Remove the skin. Add 1 cup of milk slowly to skim milk powder. Combine skim milk, warm milk and yoghurt. Put in a jar and leave to set in a warm place. Alternatively, pour into a wide-mouthed thermos flask. When set, store in the refrigerator.
Yoghurt provides the base for many sauces such as Raita and is an excellent addition to both bland and spicy dishes and soups. Chop or slice fresh pineapple, mango, pawpaw or other tropical fruits to make your own fruit yoghurt.

Low Fat Yoghurt
Use skim milk instead of full cream milk

Thick Yoghurt

2 cups milk
1 cup of skim milk powder
4 tablespoons commercial or home-made yoghurt

Prepare as for plain yoghurt

GHEE (Clarified butter)

Ghee is widely used in Asian cooking. It is a pure butter fat with no milk solids and can therefore be heated to a higher temperature than ordinary butter without burning.
Ghee is generally bought in bottles or tins. It can also be prepared at home by heating butter till it becomes frothy. Spoon off the froth and pour the melted butter into a bowl and allow to cool. Remove the fat, reheat it and strain through muslin.

TAMARIND

Tamarind is a date-like acid fruit used to give a delicate acid flavour to many Asian dishes. It is bought in pulp form from most food importers. Lemon juice is the nearest substitute if tamarind is not available.

RICE COOKING

When cooked correctly, rice should be light and fluffy in appearance. Badly cooked rice can spoil the texture and presentation of your otherwise delicious meal. Here are two well proven methods of cooking rice.

1. The Asian way is to wash the rice and then put it in a pot, adding 2 cups of water for every cup of rice. Add salt to taste and bring to the boil. Boil for five minutes, cover with a lid and steam over a very low heat until the grains are soft. Loosen with a fork.

2. Alternatively, boil 8 cups of water and sprinkle 1 cup of washed rice into the boiling water. Boil for about 10 minutes or till just soft. Strain, wash in cold water and then steam over a pot of boiling water in a colander to make it more fluffy.

BANANA LEAF COOKING

The banana leaf provides an ideal covering for cooking food by helping to retain the flavour and juices of fish, chicken, beef and vegetables. Banana leaves also impart a special flavour of their own which cannot be achieved when aluminium foil is used as a substitute.

Preparing the leaf
To prepare a leaf for wrapping food, first select a young whole leaf. With a sharp knife slice off the thick vein on the back and then hold the leaf over a flame or hot coals. Move it backwards and forwards till soft and pliable. Wrap the food in the leaf and tie with cotton or a strip of fibre made from the sliced off leaf vein.

COCONUT COOKING

The coconut shell makes an ideal cooking container. Cut the top off the coconut. This requires some expertise. Take a heavy knife and tap the round base of the section to be removed and then lift off. If you want an even top, cut around with a sharp saw. Scrape out part of the flesh from the inside and the ''lid''. Put the food inside, seal with the lid, place the nut on a stand made from an old nut shell and steam or bake. This is an interesting and delicious way to serve chicken or seafood (see recipe for Crab Vakasoso). Afterwards, clean the shells and keep for future use.

HOW TO OPEN A FRESH COCONUT

A fresh coconut should feel heavy in the hand and contain some juice. The fibrous shell should be dry, particularly round the 'eyes' at one end of the shell.
To open, firstly drain all the juice

from the coconut by piercing an 'eye' with a skewer. The juice may be drunk straight away or kept to make coconut cream.

Place the coconut in a hot oven (250º C) (475º F) for about 10 minutes till the outer shell cracks. Remove from oven and tap the shell with the back of a heavy chopper or hammer. The shell will break into smaller pieces and the coconut meat should lift out easily using the point of a knife. Quickly plunge the white meat into cold water to prevent it from cooking. If desired, the brown outer skin on the white meat may be peeled off with a potato peeler or knife.

HOW TO MAKE COCONUT CREAM

Coconut cream is an essential ingredient of many tropical recipes. It is best made from fresh coconuts, but is also available in cans from most supermarkets.

To make fresh cream, place the flesh of one coconut in a blender jar with 2 cups of milk or water and blend at high speed until coconut is completely pulverised. The richness of coconut cream is determined by the amount of water added to the grated flesh. For a thicker cream use less water. Strain out the rich cream through muslin or a fine sieve. Save the coconut and return to blender with another cup of milk or water. Blend and strain into another bowl. This is the second extract or thin milk. Unless recipe specifies 'thick' or 'thin' milk, use both extracts combined.

If an electric blender is not available, grate the white flesh finely and to each cup of grated coconut, add ½ cup of hot water. Leave to cool, then knead firmly and strain out the liquid. Repeat the process a second and even third time.

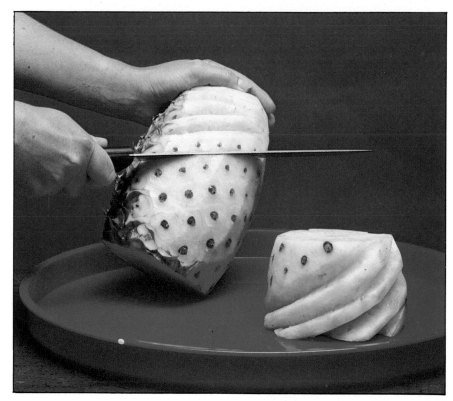

How to cut a fresh pineapple

A Hint When Using Coconut Cream

Coconut cream contains some protein. When boiled the protein curdles and separates out. This does not matter in some dishes, but in other recipes such as fish soup, the consistency and flavour are spoiled by boiling the cream. The addition of a little cornflour helps to prevent curdling, however it is best to cook the majority of coconut cream dishes at simmering point.

Grated Coconut

Fresh coconut may be grated on a hand grater, or broken into pieces and put into a food processor with a stainless steel chopping blade. Using an electric food processor will give you a finer ground. Add a little liquid to the blender as this will facilitate the grinding. Blend to the consistency you want. For cake and dessert toppings it is best not to grind coconut too finely. Grated coconut will keep for two weeks in the fridge or for several months in the freezer.

HOW TO CUT A FRESH PINEAPPLE

Firstly cut off the top and base of the pineapple and peel off the outer skin with a sharp knife. Then, starting at the top, make parallel cuts in the form of a wedge on each side of the 'eyes' working down around the pineapple in a spiral manner. When completed there should be a series of 'ridges' running round from top to bottom with no 'eyes' left.

The pineapple is now ready to slice or dice, depending on how you wish to serve it.

Handy Measurements

The correct use and understanding of measurements will ensure good cooking results. With the conversion to metric measures, it is important to understand and use the new metric measures in cooking. To help you we have made this a metric cookbook. Always remember when measuring that results will be correct as long as all metric or all imperial measures are used. Don't use a combination of them both and always use level measures.

MEASURING ABBREVIATIONS

t	teaspoon	C	celsius
T	tablespoon	F	fahrenheit
c	cup	ml	millilitre
lb	pound	l	litre
oz	ounce	cm	centimetre
g	gram	mm	millimetre
kg	kilogram		

2 teaspoons = 1 dessertspoon
2 dessertspoons = 1 tablespoon

DRY MEASURES

½ oz	15 gm	9 oz	285 gm
1 oz	30 gm	10 oz	315 gm
2 oz	60 gm	11 oz	345 gm
3 oz	90 gm	12 oz	375 gm
4 oz	125 gm		
		13 oz	405 gm
5 oz	155 gm	14 oz	440 gm
6 oz	185 gm	15 oz	470 gm
7 oz	220 gm	16 oz (1 lb)	500 gm
8 oz	250 gm	2 lb	1 kg

LIQUID OR VOLUME MEASURE

1 teaspoon	5 ml
1 dessertspoon	10 ml
1 tablespoon	20 ml (Australia)
1 tablespoon	15 ml (NZ)
1 fluid ounce	30 ml
½ cup (4 fl oz)	125 ml
¼ pint (5 fl oz)	250 ml
½ pint (10 fl oz)	300 ml
1½ cups (12 fl oz)	375 ml
2 metric cups	500 ml
1 pint (20 fl oz)	600 ml
4 metric cups	1000 ml or 1 litre
35 fl oz	1000 ml or 1 litre
1¾ pints	1000 ml or 1 litre

OVEN TEMPERATURES

	F.	C.	GAS
	200	100	¼
Very Slow	220	110	½
	250	120	¾
Slow	275	140	3
	300	150	2
Moderately Slow	325	160	3
Moderate	350	180	4
Moderately Hot	375	190	5
	400	200	6
Hot	425	220	7
Very Hot	450	230	8
	475	250	9

Index

Right: Preparation of beef kovu